A PASSION FOR COOPERATION

CAMPUS VOICES

STORIES OF EXCELLENCE FROM THE UNIVERSITY OF MICHIGAN

Books in the Series

A PASSION FOR COOPERATION

Adventures of a Wide-Ranging Scientist

Robert Axelrod

University of Michigan Press
Ann Arbor

For questions or permissions, please contact um.press.perms@umich.edu

Published in the United States of America by the
University of Michigan Press
Manufactured in the United States of America
Printed on acid-free paper
First published November 2023

A CIP catalog record for this book is available from the British Library.

Library of Congress Cataloging-in-Publication data has been applied for.

ISBN 978-0-472-07655-0 (hardcover : alk. paper)
ISBN 978-0-472-05655-2 (paper : alk. paper)
ISBN 978-0-472-90394-8 (e-book)

To my grandchild Aviva

CONTENTS

PART IV. SELF-ORGANIZATION

PART V. SEX AND CANCER

PART VI. OUTSIDE THE IVORY TOWER

PART VII. CONCLUDING THOUGHTS

Digital materials related to this title can be found
on the Fulcrum platform via the following citable URL:
https://doi.org/10.3998/mpub.12760872

ILLUSTRATIONS

FOREWORD

One day in 1982, during my three-year stint as a columnist for the venerable magazine *Scientific American*, I received a package (it was, after all, the snail-mail era) from a professor of political science at the University of Michigan named Robert Axelrod. The package contained a letter plus a book in draft form. In his letter, Prof. Axelrod described an abstract game played with numbers called "Prisoner's Dilemma" (PD for short), which fascinated me because of its quasi-paradoxical nature. In a nutshell, the angelic side of your nature wants to *cooperate* with the other player, as mutual cooperation will bring you both three points—but a sly little devil whispers in your ear that *not* cooperating—technically called *defecting*—will bring you five big ones (provided the other player cooperates, in which case they will get zilch). But if you *both* defect, each of you gets just one measly little point. Damn!

What to do? Cooperate and hope your partner does too, but also risk getting nothing at all? Or defect and hope for five points, but also risk getting only one? It's a tricky dilemma, and the more you think about it, the trickier it gets. And what strategy to follow if you're playing many games in a row with the same partner (or should I say "adversary"?), and can react instantly to their behavior? Prof. Axelrod explained in his letter that he'd recently conducted a PD tournament in which over sixty computer programs had all vied with one another, over a couple of hundred rounds of this game, to come out with the highest total score. To his great surprise, it was the very simplest strategy—a nearly trivial strategy called TIT FOR TAT—that had emerged victorious. TIT FOR TAT always opens angelically by cooperating, and thereafter it merely echoes whatever its frenemy did last time.

The manuscript that Prof. Axelrod had enclosed gave details in a very lucid fashion, and in conclusion he politely asked whether I would consider writing about his computer tournament in one of my "Metamagical Themas" columns. It was such a thought-provoking topic that I couldn't resist, so in May 1983 I wrote my column on the Prisoner's Dilemma, on the tournament, on various rival strategies, and on why TIT FOR TAT was so successful. In writing it, though, I unexpectedly got so hooked on the PD that I wound up devoting my June column to variations on the theme, and in it I even announced my own worldwide tournament of a related numbers-game that I called the "Luring Lottery," on whose results I reported in my September column. The PD and its close cousins, including the "Tragedy of the Commons," became one of the most engrossing topics I had ever encountered.

Not long after that, a small cabal of professors at the University of Michigan collectively invited me to join them on the faculty there. That would mean leaving Indiana University, which had been my warm home for seven years. But these four professors—Arthur Burks (philosopher and mathematician), Richard Nisbett (cognitive psychologist), John Holland (computer scientist and lifelong student of evolution), and Robert Axelrod (political scientist and game theorist)—were all highly original thinkers whose intellectual company would be hard to match. After serious deliberation, I made the pivotal decision to join them in Michigan.

I'll never forget my first visit to Ann Arbor, nearly forty years ago, when I got to know Bob Axelrod and his sparklingly lively wife, Amy Saldinger. They hospitably put me up in their home, and ever since then, we have all remained close. Over the years, Bob and Amy's friendship has grown ever more precious to me.

I carefully read the early version of Bob's book and thought it was as good as gold, and so, to help him get it into print, I put him in touch with my publisher, Martin Kessler, at Basic Books in New York. Kessler was quickly persuaded of the depth and power of Bob's ideas, and it wasn't long before *The Evolution of Cooperation* appeared, and it made quite a splash. In fact, it has become a classic text—truly a beautiful and deep contribution to thought about how life works.

Fast forward roughly thirty years. When Bob turned seventy, there was a splendid celebratory event in Ann Arbor that I attended, and I heard talk after talk by Bob's former doctoral students and other colleagues explaining the extraordinary variety of Bob's research projects over several decades. I was bowled over, as I had been entirely unaware of the richness and breadth of his non-PD research. I also was most amused when, at the very end, Bob himself gave a short, modest talk in which he told the assembled crowd some of his "life principles" that he'd distilled into short and punchy maxims. One of my favorites was this one: "Don't ever teach a course for the first time." What a gem of a quip, and it has so much truth to it!

During a question-and-answer session, I brought up a point that I think might be interesting to mention here. In Bob's computer PD tournaments, the inanimate programs of course had no feelings of empathy; they were all just trying to outscore other programs, and yet, most strikingly, it turned out that pure self-interest led to the dominance of a TIT FOR TAT-ish type of cooperative behavior. I felt, however, that Bob's approach left out one key source of *human* cooperation, which is that we humans can't help *identifying* with other creatures (usually other humans, even fictional ones); we care about them because we feel we live partly inside them, and they live partly inside us. Many humans feel this way also about pets, sometimes even about stuffed animals! We project ourselves naturally into others and do kind deeds for them, without ever expecting to gain anything from so doing.

In my question to Bob, I asked whether this kind of human behavior was a different type of cooperation requiring a different type of explanation. An example I cited was late one night when I'd bought something at a twenty-four-hour convenience store and walked out, overlooking a $20 bill on the counter, which was most of my change. The clerk dashed out the door and presented me—a total stranger—with the $20 bill. Perhaps he didn't want me to feel pain at some later point when I checked my wallet and saw the lack of $20 that I should have had. Or maybe he didn't even think I would ever notice the absence of a $20 bill, but he simply felt that it belonged to me, and he didn't want me to be deprived of something that was mine. My question to Bob concerned what he thought about such acts of kindness toward other sentient beings—acts that come out of identification of oneself with others, rather than out of unconscious inbuilt strategies that evolved in the billion-year-old story of merciless dog-eat-dog evolutionary competition.

In his answer, Bob stated that programs that play the iterated PD are egoists seeking only to maximize their scores, and are thus by definition not altruists. What fascinated him was the thorny question of how cooperation could emerge even among egotists. However, he agreed that in actual human life, altruistic acts are important, and can take place even between strangers.

A couple of years ago, Bob told me that he had started writing a memoir of his adventurous life. I was very happy to hear this news, and when he sent me a draft, I devoured it with excitement. The first couple of chapters were marvelously vivid in portraying the development of a young mind driven by insatiable curiosity and lots of self-confidence. I was surprised to learn how much he had savored intense competition and how successful he'd been at it. For instance, as a high school senior he won a Westinghouse Fellowship, one of just five in the country, and was welcomed to the White House by President John F. Kennedy. At that time, young Bob wrote an amazingly prescient statement about his own future, hinting at many of the paths he subsequently followed. In reading these early chapters of the book, I got a kick out of coming to know Bob as an adolescent, and could easily imagine how we might have been great friends had we known each other way back then.

At the University of Chicago, Bob took courses not just in math and political science (his top loves) but also in the humanities, thereby becoming a lifelong fan of impressionism and of classical music. I was amused to read, however, that for a while he semibelieved that the distinction between major and minor in music was just a hoax concocted in order to make him look foolish.

During his college years, Bob spent a summer at the Hudson Institute, a think tank founded by nuclear-war theorist Herman Kahn. As Bob puts it, "It didn't bother me that I was a liberal dove and he was a conservative hawk." Such open-mindedness is so typical of Bob's style. For instance, in 1969, at the height of the Vietnam War, Bob was one of the organizers of the Moratorium Against the Vietnam War, a major protest in Washington, DC. And yet, in order to make it come off smoothly, he met and cooperated in a civil manner not only with officials from the Washington, DC Police Department but also with representatives from the Nixon White House!

A pervasive theme of Bob's life is that he has not just wanted to *understand* the world, but also has always had a deep desire to *make a difference, however small*. Ever since his late teenage years, when he was so deeply struck by the very frightening Cuban Missile Crisis, he has yearned to contribute to making the world a better and more secure place. In fact, he declares, "My game theory work on cooperation was initially motivated by a search for ways in which two egoistic actors, such as the United States and the Soviet Union, could avoid conflict."

Not just an ivory tower theorizer on the evolution of cooperation, Bob has long striven to practice what he preaches. He has traveled far and worked hard to try to reduce tensions in serious conflicts in diverse regions of the world, ranging from arms control involving the US and the Soviet Union, to the United Nations peacekeeping efforts in the shattered area once known as Yugoslavia, to the ever-fluctuating, unpredictable tension between Israelis and Palestinians. Thanks to his prominence as an advocate of cooperation and also to his nonconfrontational stance, Bob has been able to meet with powerful individuals of radically different cultures and belief systems, such as Iran's president Mahmoud Ahmadinejad, Israel's prime minister Benjamin Netanyahu, and the leaders of several Palestinian organizations, including Hamas, Islamic Jihad, and the Popular Front for the Liberation of Palestine. Although all these individuals belong to severely clashing religious and ethnic groups, Bob has managed to conduct civil and productive discussions with them, and has done his best to find common ground and has sought creative ways to forge agreements, no matter how inflexible and hard-line such people's public pronouncements might have been.

All of this hard work to try to *make a difference, however small*, has taken great physical and intellectual courage, but it has paid off, in that Bob's academic work and his practical work have complemented and enriched each other: his game-theoretical research into cooperation has enabled him to meet with and make suggestions to people in positions of high power, thus changing the world for the better, and his interactions with them have in turn helped him to refine and generalize his theoretical understanding of how cooperation can evolve.

I've now read Bob's adventures a few times, and I've always found that the later chapters in the book are considerably tougher going than the earlier ones, as they describe many facets of his scientific research and his idealistic political work using language that I am not very familiar with, but each time, when I've stepped back and taken a broader view, I've found them exhilarating, a bit like viewing a spectacular mountain range from afar.

If I were in a position to do so (which I certainly am not), I would nominate Bob for a Nobel Prize in economics, because his research on the emergence of cooperation and organization has shed such important light on how societies work, ranging all the way from cancer cells to insects to human beings. But even if the Nobel Committee hasn't yet seen the light, the MacArthur Foundation saw it a long time ago, in awarding him one of its coveted Genius Grants, and so did President Barack Obama, in awarding him a National Medal of Science. Such recognitions were deeply deserved. After all, it's not every scientist whose articles have been cited over 90,000 times. This is an enormously large figure, and yet it gives only the slightest hint of how huge has been the influence of Bob's manifold discoveries on our scientific understanding of how cooperation and organization can spontaneously emerge from competition.

I am proud to be a close friend of someone so brilliant and simultaneously so humble, and I am so glad that Bob chose to share with the world the story of the development of his inquisitive mind, his ingenious ideas, his wide-ranging research program, and his ever-fresh attempts to make a difference, however small. He is the very rare sort of scientist whose impact on numerous disciplines will reverberate down the generations, and I hope that this little book will not only fascinate many readers, but will inspire younger readers to join in the exploration of the vast and intricately crisscrossing world of intellectual pathways that Bob, cooperating with his students and colleagues, has revealed and opened up.

Douglas Hofstadter
February 2023

A SPLENDID EDUCATION

CHAPTER 1

FAMILY, MATH, AND COMPETITIVENESS

My brother Dave and I were the first in our family to go to college.

Our mother, Rose, was born in Warsaw in 1913. When World War I broke out, her father mutilated his trigger finger so that he would not have to use a gun to fight. He was drafted into the czarist army anyway. As one of the few literate soldiers in his unit, he became the company clerk. In 1920 he picked up his family and moved to the United States, settling on the West Side of Chicago. Had he not emigrated, he and the rest of his family would been wiped out in the Holocaust, as were so many of his relatives who stayed behind.

Much later, Dave asked Grandpa Charles, "Did you really think that the streets in America were paved with gold?" He responded, "It was better than that. In Poland parents could be arrested for trying to get their child into school. In America parents could get arrested if they did not bring their child to school."

In the United States, my mom's childhood was very difficult. With her parents and two younger sisters, she lived behind their parents' delicatessen. The living quarters were divided from the store by primitive three-quarter-height partitions, not regular walls. Every sound from the store came into where they lived, and consequently there was no privacy or quiet. A sheet divided the living room from the bedroom area, which was itself subdivided by another sheet beyond which lay the toilet and a large tin enameled tub. Living in such a closed space and working long hours, her parents bickered a lot, which couldn't have been easy on my mom.

School too was hard for my mom: she arrived as a seven year old with no knowledge of English and an undiagnosed severe near-sightedness. At grammar school she was placed in a room for the "Handicapped," where she was set to work making pot holders, paper cutouts, and drawings. Immigrants with three small children, struggling to make ends meet in their "ma and pa store," her parents had neither the time nor the knowledge to sort things out at school. Her true problem remained undiscovered until another greenhorn, a nineteen-year-old cousin—incredulous that this lively and seemingly intelligent little girl could not be taught to read or write—took her to Hull House, which was one of the country's first private settlement houses that served the needy including recent emigrants. Hull House provided her with her first pair of glasses. Putting them on, she recalled that the world seemed to hit her in the face.

My mother had a deep sense of curiosity. She was an avid reader with a wide range of interests such as comparative religion and current events. She eventually earned enough credits in adult education classes to have the equivalent of a college degree. She was ambitious for her sons and was very proud when both became professors.

My father, James, was a second-generation American who grew up in Chicago as one of eight children. His father was an Orthodox Jew who owned a small tailor shop. Like my mother's family, both sides of my father's family came from eastern Europe: Minsk on his father's side, and the small town of Milawa in Poland on his mother's side.

My father developed an early love of drawing and painting in watercolors. He made a modest living at it by becoming a commercial artist, usually bringing work home in the evening. This gave him the opportunity to create art, albeit art produced for advertisements. If someone had asked Dad to describe himself professionally, he'd have said, "I'm a freelance artist." The "freelance" part was very important. Dad valued his freedom and independence. He never had a steady income or knew where the next month's job would come from, or even whether there *would* be a job next month. For someone who grew up in the Depression, this required a great deal of courage: a strong belief in himself, as well as an optimism that things would work out.

While commercial art was his bread and butter, his real love was watercolors. He loved to paint boats, intricate trees, Chicago scenes, Jewish themes, and especially farms. As a kid, I was fascinated to see him explore the countryside looking for a typical farm, and I would watch him paint his version of it. The cows might turn out purple, but under the shade of a tree, they would look like they *ought* to be purple. From my dad I learned of the possibility of earning a living doing what you want to do, as well as the fulfillment that comes from creative expression. I learned from Dad that work can be joyful, that work can be play, that work can be a form of self-expression. And that work can be inspiring, giving pleasure not only to oneself, but to others as well. I also learned from seeing that he never had an unkind word to say about anyone.

My parents had a wonderful marriage, being totally devoted to each other. They lived in a small apartment, where Dave and I shared the one bedroom, and my parents slept on a foldout couch in the living room. Although we were not rich in wealth, we were rich in care and compassion.

I often heard Mom complain to Dad about minor things, and she frequently tried to get me to take her side. As a child, I couldn't stand it. Much later, I realized that much of the problem was that my mother regretted that my dad remained a freelance artist rather than starting an ad agency so he could build a business. His staying self-employed meant that although he worked long hours they couldn't keep up with their high school peers who had gone on to professional careers in fields such as law, business, and medicine. Perhaps their arguing, minor as it was, was the beginning of my lifelong drive to understand how to promote cooperation.

To my brother, Dave, who was three years older than me, I must have been quite a pest, since I always wanted to follow him to play with him and his friends. I always wanted to do everything he could do—and, if possible, do it better. Although I was competitive with him, he was always supportive of me. It took me about fifty years to get over it. (But more on that later.)

My earliest memory of competitiveness goes back to when I was about thirteen. The teacher gave our class the challenge of coming up with the most words that could be spelled with the letters of "constitutional." We had one week. I and some others came up with a few dozen words in the first day. But then I realized that I'd have to do something systematic to win. So I got a large dictionary and went through it page by page. It didn't take as long I had first expected, since I could skip sections with R or E, for example. As I recall, I found about 700 words that week, easily winning the contest and getting the promised prize—a nicely illustrated book I could show off to the class. I discovered that a little diligence could go a long way.

When my parents were able to move from their one-bedroom apartment in Chicago, they bought a small house in the suburb of Evanston because of its excellent public schools. My first joy of seeing beauty in mathematics came at age thirteen while I was learning a form of symbolic logic called Boolean algebra. I saw that Boolean algebra was simpler and more elegant than regular algebra. For example, I was particularly impressed that, in Boolean algebra, addition distributes over multiplication as well as vice versa.[1] I felt like someone who had just gotten a glimpse of previously unimagined possibilities and wonders beyond their one village.

When my mom realized that I was interested in math, she suggested I might become a certified public accountant. I didn't know how to explain to her that what attracted me to math was abstraction and beauty, and I didn't see that in accounting.

In retrospect, I see a connection between my father's process of creating a new visual representation of a scene and a mathematician's process of developing beautiful new math. I came to see my later work in math modeling as analogous to my father's watercolors. In both pursuits, the idea was to represent something in a new way that displayed an interesting conception of reality by focusing on some of its aspects and setting aside other aspects that would get in the way of appreciating what this new view of things has to offer.

From about the same time, I distinctly remember a middle school assignment to find out what the police and firefighters of Evanston thought about a proposal to give them cross-training. It seemed like a very sensible idea to me. I called one of the local fire stations and asked the person who picked up the phone what he thought about the cross-training plan. While memory isn't reliable, I can still recall the answer I got: "I don't know anything about that, but we're all against it down here." This was my first research project and it made an impression on me because I learned a lot. I learned that (a) what I thought was a good idea might not seem at all good to the people involved, (b) one can have an opinion without information, and (c) if the opinion is based on the opinion of others who share one's values, it may not be so silly after all.

For leisure on Saturdays I would often go the John Crerar Library in downtown Chicago. The library specialized in science, technology, and medicine. Amid its open shelves I was free to explore to my heart's content. I recall reading military magazines, the British humor magazine *Punch*, and both *Popular Mechanics* and *Popular Science* magazines. It was the start of my lifelong habit of browsing a wide variety of journals and magazines, and learning about interesting things I hadn't known even existed.

On a less pleasant note, the anxiety of the Cold War was brought home to me as a twelve year old in 1955 when our school had a civil defense drill in which we cowered under our desks in anticipation of nuclear war.

CHAPTER 2

COMPUTERS AND MODELING

I had the very good fortune of attending Evanston Township High School, one of the best public high schools in the nation. While there, I tried out all sorts of things to see what I would like and what I was good at: debate, chess, student government, math, and even wrestling. I found the most success in math, becoming captain of the math team that won second place in a national competition sponsored by the Future Engineers of America.

I wasn't much of an athlete, but I was told that the varsity wrestling team desperately needed someone who would qualify for the ninety-five-pound category. As I was slight of build, I fit the bill; as it turned out, though, I wasn't much help after all. But something fun came out of it when I became intrigued by the drops of condensed perspiration falling from the ceiling and splattering onto the slick mats below. After leaving the wrestling team, I started playing around with an eyedropper, squeezing one drop of colored water at a time onto a sheet of paper from a height of several feet. After the drops dried, I measured their diameter on the paper and saw how their size systematically varied with the height from which I dropped them. I was also curious about whether a thicker liquid would change the size of the splatter, so I mixed the water with measured amounts of glycerin. After measuring several hundred dried spots on paper, I was able to plot the diameter of the spot as a function of the height from which it was dropped and the percentage of the thickening agent. The result was a series of regular curves that showed the effect on the size of the splatter due to the interaction between the height of the drop and the thickness of the liquid. I then turned this into a science fair exhibit. Searching for some application, I offered the not-too-impressive claim that this method could be used to measure the viscosity of a liquid without having to do any mechanical measures with a well-calibrated stirring device. It seems that, even as a high school sophomore, I wanted to find a practical application for my observations.

I received a top award in the Illinois State Science Fair and an extraordinary letter from one of the judges: "You saw there were laws to be uncovered in the familiar phenomena of falling drops. The ability to see regularity where others do not is the major quality which distinguishes the great scientist from his fellow beings."

I've always enjoyed the challenge of intellectual competition. This urge was especially strong in high school. At that time, I entered many math and science competitions. I also worked hard to earn good grades on tests and a strong overall grade point average. I even compared my SAT scores with my peers in the honors courses I took. Overall, I saw myself as virtually never at the top, but always pretty close. For example, I graduated twelfth of 800 students, and I never got a perfect 800 on any SAT exam, while more than half of my peers did. The challenge provided by the twenty or so high school classmates in these college prep courses was the toughest daily competition among a small group of friends that I've ever had throughout my education and subsequent career.

In high school, I had a history teacher who had been an assistant professor at Northwestern University. He told my class that the American Historical Association was holding its annual meeting in Chicago, and high school students would be welcome to sit in on any of the presentations. Being curious about what academic research looked like, I went, and I heard a talk about using the statistics of word usage to attribute specific Federalist Papers to one of the three possible authors based on their known writings. I liked the idea of using quantitative analysis to answer interesting political questions. It was my first exposure to the academic world, and I liked what I saw.

An important move in my life came when Steve Crocker, my good friend and fellow math enthusiast, invited me to join him in teaching ourselves how to program a computer. I accepted his challenge with glee. This would have been in the fall of 1959 when we were juniors in high school. With Steve's playfulness and infectious enthusiasm we became lifelong friends. Steve went on to an illustrious career as one of the pioneers in developing what became the internet. One of his most helpful contributions was the founding of the "Request for Comments" series that served as the mechanism for achieving global consensus for how diverse computers should communicate with each other. Although he is too modest to admit it, he helped establish the cooperative culture that was vital to the rapid progress of scaling up the early small early network of computers at a handful of universities to the five billion users of the internet today. Steve was so successful at building trust that he was elected to chair the board of ICANN, the global organization that helps coordinate the allocation and assignment of the internet's addresses and domain names.

When Steve and I learned programming, Northwestern University had only one computer. The head of the computer center was Professor Harry Rymer of the Astronomy Department. When I asked if I could work there, he graciously offered me a summer internship with a token salary and an easy assignment to get started. Since the computer could handle only one task at a time, there was a signup sheet for fifteen-minute blocks. The IBM 650 and its related equipment filled much of a large room of the university observatory but had only 8,000 memory addresses (compared to billions in today's laptops). With so little memory, programming was a demanding art. When I did get a chance to run a program, something almost always went wrong, at which point I would analyze the problem, rush to the card punch to make a correction in my stack of cards, and try again before my fifteen minutes were up. It was hectic, but also a lot of fun. I loved the challenge of figuring out how to tell the computer to go about solving a particular problem, and I was pleased when I had eliminated all the bugs in my program and saw that it actually worked. Moreover, I liked the similarity to theorem proving in which the result had no room for ambiguity. Best of all, I got a feeling of empowerment when the computer did what I told it to do. While at the computer center, I started my lifelong habit of periodically scanning a wide range of academic journals to see what might be interesting. An article in the *IBM Journal of Research and Development* caught my attention because it described a computer program that could independently learn to play checkers so well that it could beat the person who programmed it.[2] That article led me to follow the literature on computer programs to play chess, and I was intrigued by the tournaments that were organized to evaluate their performance.

One of the side benefits of working at the observatory was a chance to take part in an all-night effort to share in the making of history. On August 12, 1960, the United States launched the ECHO satellite, hoping to achieve success after a series of American rocket failures following the launch of the first *Sputnik*. The ECHO satellite was a Mylar balloon designed to inflate to a diameter of one hundred feet—big enough to allow radio signals to be transmitted from Earth and reflected back across great distances. The question was whether the balloon would really inflate upon reaching its hundred-mile-high orbit. At it happened, Northwestern's observatory had the nation's (and perhaps the world's) largest telescope that could manually track a satellite. All larger telescopes allowed only mechanical steering designed to compensate for the slow rotation of the Earth itself. Our team at Northwestern was able to track and photograph the ECHO satellite on its first night. We developed the film, measured the size of the image, and claimed that we were the first to confirm that the ECHO satellite had, indeed, fully expanded. Early the next morning, we proudly took our photos to Professor Rymer, hoping he'd authorize a public announcement of our accomplishment. Instead, he took one look at the photos and sadly informed us that we couldn't determine the size of the satellite since the image itself was so small as to be indistinguishable from a single dot on the film. The lesson I took to heart from this disappointment was that it would have been helpful for our team to have thought through the exercise before wasting our time on what would inevitably be an indeterminate result, given the equipment we had. I expect that this little lesson helped save me a lot of unnecessary work in the years ahead.

I had a marvelous high school teacher, Murl Salisbury, who did wonders by doing almost nothing. He offered a course spread over two semesters on doing research in science. On the first day, he explained to us that for the first semester we should take turns presenting some interesting research topics; in the second semester we should take turns presenting our own research projects. He would be in the room next door in case we needed him, but otherwise we were on our own. He provided the opportunity for us to discover the power of collaboration and the joy of discovering something new on our own. And it worked. Everyone really did develop original research projects. Over time, the Evanston Township High School produced more winners of the Westinghouse National Science Talent Search than almost any other school in the country.

For my project, I took advantage of my access to Northwestern's only computer. I decided to play around by developing a simulation of hypothetical life forms and environments. The idea was inspired by my pet, a baby alligator, who lived in a washtub and scrounged around looking for food. The simulation involved trying a range of strategies that an animal could use to search its neighborhood for food. The best strategy turned out to be one that had a way to exploit clues in the environment about where the food was likely to be found. I submitted the project to the Westinghouse competition and was named one of the forty most promising young scientists in the country.

One lesson I took away from that experience is that playfulness can sometimes be quite productive. Another lesson was that computers could be great toys. I especially enjoyed using them to simulate something, and then being delighted when the output revealed a fascinating surprise. But the most important result of my success with my Westinghouse science project was that it helped give me the confidence that would prove so helpful throughout my career.

A reward for being selected in the Westinghouse competition was a trip to Washington and a chance to compete for one of five college scholarships. The selection process included one interview with a scientist and another with a psychologist. I can't remember what the psychologist asked, but I vividly remember being stumped by a question from the scientist: "How can we find out if the moon's surface is solid enough for a future astronaut to walk on?" My mind was racing because the answer might determine whether or not I would get a four-year scholarship. But I couldn't think of anything I knew that could be at all relevant to what the surface of the moon was like. To gain time, I asked, "How much money do we have?" The judge said, "Say, a million dollars." To that I replied, "Well, in that case the only thing you can afford would be a survey of the relevant experts to see what they thought." I was rather proud of that answer, or at least my turning it from a physics or mechanical engineering question—about which I knew precious little—to a social science question about which I had at least heard of surveys. It was the first but certainly not the last time I dealt with a problem in a given discipline with tools from another discipline.

I was ranked sixth, but fortunately, one of the students who was ranked higher than I was declined the Westinghouse scholarship to take a different one. He was Dan Kleinman, who left mathematics after college to become a successful screenwriter. We became lifelong friends.

During the gathering in Washington, DC, each of the forty finalists was asked to write a few paragraphs describing the most-needed scientific discovery, and how we envisioned our career. Although it was written in 1961 when I was still in high school, my response foreshadowed much of my career.

The most needed science discovery today is information leading to an understanding of the way in which a human arrives at a decision. An understanding of a person's thinking process would have vast implications in the social sciences and might enable us to make advancements in such vital areas as political science.

I believe that the greatest promise for success in understanding the human mind lies in the three fields of psychology, physiology, and artificial intelligence. It seems to me that in the next few years great advances will be made through investigation into the characteristics of simulated intelligence.

I would like to contribute to science by being a part of a research team working to advance the frontiers of pure science. At the present time, however, I cannot be absolutely certain that I will enter a scientific career, but if I do, it will probably be as a mathematician working with a group which combines two or more branches of science. I have selected this work because I believe that the greatest advances in the next quarter century will be derived from the uniting of two previously independent studies, such as mathematics and biology.

Figure 1. In the Oval Office, March 6, 1961

As I read now what I wrote at seventeen years old, I am struck by how much it foretold. I did indeed move from math in college to what I considered to be the vital field of political science in graduate school. Later I applied my math to evolutionary biology. I also became fascinated by artificial intelligence for games of strategy, and then conducted my own computer tournaments. I fulfilled my hope of working in interdisciplinary groups, one of which included people from five or more disciplines and stayed active for more than twenty-five years. I also did research in psychology, including the coherence of belief systems and the basis for ethnocentrism. As for physiology, I had an idea about cooperation among tumor cells that led to an extensive collaboration with cancer researchers. I still find it hard to believe that I wound up over the next sixty years doing research on the wide range of interests I identified in high school.

The biggest thrill of the Washington trip was a visit to the Oval Office to be received by the recently inaugurated and very charming President

John F. Kennedy. Like many others, I was inspired by the challenge he issued at his inauguration three months earlier: "Ask not what your country can do for you. Ask what you can do for your country." Now he kidded around with our group by pointing out how he enjoyed hearing that most of us wanted to go to some small college in Massachusetts. I was certainly one of those aspirants. What made the biggest impression on me, however, was my strong sense of sympathy for Vice President Lyndon Johnson, who had, until recently, been the forceful leader of the Senate. In the Oval Office, Johnson seemed like a caged lion who was struggling to play second fiddle to someone else. No doubt, my empathy was evoked by my feelings with having had to play second fiddle to my older brother.

President Kennedy was in a great mood. Years later, I learned that, shortly before seeing us, he had given final approval for the Bay of Pigs invasion to overthrow his nemesis, Fidel Castro. The invasion turned out to be a fiasco. Many years later, when I met President Obama at another awards ceremony in the White House, I wanted to suggest that he not do anything rash that day. But I didn't get the chance.

CHAPTER 3

CULTURE AND MORE MATH AT COLLEGE

After the incredible high of the week in Washington with the Westinghouse winners, I received a thin envelope from Harvard with a notice of my rejection. I felt like I was a racehorse at an auction where no one wanted to bid on me since I was deemed to be worthless. It was quite a blow.

Fortunately my other three applications resulted in acceptances from Princeton, Cornell, and the University of Chicago. Princeton had the best math department, but at an alumni recruitment event a recruiter spoke with disdain of "the nerd at the end of the hall," giving me the distinct impression that studious undergrads were seen as social isolates of little value to the rest of the student body. Cornell had a beautiful setting, but the isolation of the campus put me off. I was somewhat familiar with the University of Chicago since my brother was a junior there. I felt more comfortable at a school where nerds were welcome. In retrospect, I think an additional motivation was a chance to outperform my brother on his own turf.

The recruiters for Chicago told me that students in the dorms talked about Aristotle at breakfast. And sure enough, they did. The reason is that everyone was required to take a long list of required courses, and so most of us were reading Aristotle at the same time. I loved it.

The humanities sequence introduced me to a lifelong love of impressionist art, especially van Gogh's. The section on music appreciation led to a lifelong enjoyment of classical music, but I must admit that I couldn't do much better than chance at identifying whether a given piece was in a major or a minor key. For a moment I entertained the idea that this so-called distinction was an elaborate hoax designed to make me look foolish.

While most of my friends studied India for their non-Western civilization requirement, I chose China because I was less interested in Buddhist thought than I was in world affairs, and I expected that China would be more important than India in those terms. The most memorable moment was when the instructor, Professor Harlee Creel, took us to his office to show us his personal collection of 3,500-year-old Shang vessels that he had acquired in China in the 1930s. The aesthetic conception was so refined and so different from anything I had seen before that I was enchanted and have remained so ever since. Moreover, I was amazed at the quality of the artistry from around 1500 BC, which exploited technology that was more than a thousand years ahead of its Western equivalent. I remain enchanted. I still have several reproductions prominently displayed in my home and seek them out at almost every museum I visit.

Chicago gave its own placement exams before classes started. Thanks to my high school experience, I placed out of enough of the requirements to allow me to graduate in three years. During that time, I focused on math, and I started to take graduate courses in my second year. I found math to be so fascinating that it was worth the sustained effort required. I never made much use of topology or most of the other esoteric topics I studied, but looking back on it, I realized math gave me invaluable practice in logical thinking and the development of self-discipline. I have come to see my hard work at math as something akin to long-distance running: it is nice if you can see beauty along the way, but it is also helpful for the muscles you build up—literal or figurative—as well as the experience of hard work being rewarding.

In my third year of college, I became disillusioned with the prospect of a career in mathematics and decided to pursue a PhD in political science. True, I was good at math, but I doubted I was good enough to have a distinguished career in pure math. Further, I didn't want a career that peaked in my thirties, long the conventional wisdom about math. The coup de grace was my reaction to seeing the questions asked of graduate math students on their PhD qualifying exams. While I didn't understand most of the questions (let alone be able to answer them), I could see that many took the form of "prove that all subsquate questers are quis-ters." I decided then that I didn't want to devote my career to that sort of question.

My disenchantment with a career in pure math was bolstered by my growing attraction to social science, and, with it, the idea that I could help to make a difference in the world. The Cuban Missile Crisis had occurred in my second year of college, and it left me profoundly puzzled. Why had the US risked nuclear war to prevent Soviet missiles from being installed in Cuba when the missiles could have as easily been launched from anywhere? I felt an urgency to devote my energies to examining how to lower the risk of a hundred million people dying in a nuclear war. I had no idea whether my work would amount to any real contribution, but at least I would have tried.

CHAPTER 4

INTERNSHIPS ON STATISTICS, EVOLUTION, AND NATIONAL SECURITY

IBM and Abbott Labs, 1961. As mentioned earlier, I had the opportunity to develop my programming skills as a summer intern at Northwestern's Computer Center. This led to a summer internship at IBM's office in Evanston, Illinois. This was the first of many valuable summer internships for me. This one was in the summer between high school and college. IBM assigned me to the Statistical Group of Abbott Laboratories. On my first day, my boss showed me a two-volume work called *The Advanced Theory of Statistics,* pointing me to the last two chapters, which were full of complicated formulae. My job was to write a program that would perform the kind of analysis described there. I was about to say, "Are you kidding?," but decided instead to see if I could do it. And I did. By the end of the summer, my boss, Raul Sanders, wrote a recommendation saying that I fit into his group "as one would expect of a professional person" and I "demonstrated exceptional ability to grasp and work with [the] very difficult problem of spectral analysis, with time series."

During the following school year, I used my spectral analysis program as a consultant to the Geology Department of Northwestern University for the analysis of geological field data.

Mathematical Biology, 1962. Given my interests in math and biology, my brother Dave suggested I apply for a summer job at the University of Chicago's Committee on Mathematical Biology. It was a small research center headed by Professor Nicolas Rashevsky. While there, I read Darwin's *The Origin of Species*, as well as a lot of recent genetics and evolutionary theory. I was impressed by Darwin's clarity, and by his candid admission that his theory had a serious problem. He said he couldn't understand how sexual reproduction wouldn't tend to eliminate most of the variability in a population as offspring would tend to have characteristics that were a blend of those of their parents. We now know that the problem was that Darwin thought in terms of analog mechanisms, while we now know that genetics is basically a digital process.

The summer spent studying evolution and genetics was helpful later on in many ways. Among other things, it gave me a good sense of how to think about interactions among whole populations rather than only focusing on individuals. I was intrigued, for example, by the concept of a "gene pool." The idea was that, for some purposes, you don't have to know which individual has which version of a gene, known as an "allele": you need only worry about the proportions of the different alleles in the population.

Hudson Institute, 1963 and 1964. In one of the few undergraduate political science courses I took in college, Professor Morton Kaplan asked if I would like to do an internship with Herman Kahn, a well-known defense intellectual and nuclear-war theorist best known for his book *On Thermonuclear War*. (He later became one of the inspirations for the titular character in the movie *Dr. Strangelove*.) He had a small think tank, the Hudson Institute, about forty miles north of New York City on its own estate. I thought that would be a lot of fun. It didn't bother me that I was a liberal dove and he was a conservative hawk.

I described in a letter to my parents my first meeting with Herman Kahn. He asked me if I had any ideas for projects that summer. He said that since he was sure my ideas would be unacceptable, we might as well get them out of the way so he could describe *his* plans. My first idea was to study the political motivation of Communist China's foreign policy. He said that this would be useful to me, but not to the Institute. My second idea was to study de-escalation, a problem prominent in my mind from the Cuban Missile Crisis. To my great surprise, he said, "That's a fine idea: go ahead, make that your summer's work." So I did. Several years later, when he published his book *On Escalation*, he gave me a gracious acknowledgment in the section on de-escalation.

Working with Herman Kahn and his colleagues taught me a lot about how defense intellectuals analyze a problem and how they prepare reports for their policy-making sponsors.

That summer I read to my heart's content, immersed myself in world politics, visited the wonders of New York City on weekends, and got to know some of my fellow interns. These four or five interns were a very sharp bunch. The group included Bob Jervis, who became a leading international relations scholar and the president of the American Political Science Association; Oran Young, who also became a distinguished political scientist; and David Lewis, who became a leading analytic philosopher.

Office of the Secretary of Defense, 1965. Given my interest in policy, I wanted to see how government worked. So I applied to the assistant secretary of defense's Policy Planning Office. Although the war in Vietnam was raging, I decided that if I could stay away from Vietnam issues being in the Pentagon for a summer would be a worthwhile experience. Just as I was able to benefit from being around Herman Kahn and his colleagues, I expected to benefit from being around the military officers and civilian officials in the Pentagon. Later I noticed that I am able to get along with and learn from a wide variety of people, including those with whom I disagree. For example, while working in the Pentagon, I came to respect military officers even while I hated the war the United States was fighting in Vietnam.

The selection system for the Secretary of Defense's summer intern program was something to write home about. I had naively expected that the primary selection criteria would be merit-based, only secondarily taking into account congressional recommendations. And indeed, on the surface, the selection process appeared objective, using grade point averages and awarding points for specific activities such as being editor of the school newspaper. However, the process was actually crafted to forestall objections from the 257 members of Congress whose recommendations couldn't be accommodated with the eighteen available internships. I ranked twenty-first. Fortunately, after a week on the waiting list, I was accepted. Already, I was gaining knowledge of how sausage is made in the real world.

I did a variety of things there. The most interesting was reading the daily pile of hundreds of cables from around the world and putting a paperclip on the few items that would be of interest to any of the five people in my office. For example, my boss was a former submarine captain who happened to be interested in chemical warfare, so anything related to that topic got a paperclip. After a while, I wasn't sure whether anybody was paying attention, so I had fun with a little prank: I put a paperclip on a message about negotiations over tariffs on canned fruit salad. That certainly got people's attention and reminded them of who was doing their filtering.

My office happened to be the repository for the three-year-old records of the Cuban Missile Crisis. A decade before they were declassified, I got to see the two cables from the Soviet Union in response to Kennedy's announcement of the "quarantine" of Cuba. The first was a heartfelt message agonizing that the two sides were pulling a knot tighter and tighter, which could be read as a fascinating attempt by Soviet premier Nikita Khrushchev to elicit cooperation. The second cable was a tough and impersonal hardline message. Fortunately, President Kennedy chose to ignore the second message and respond to the first.

I found the work on international security affairs to be exciting, so I was surprised when I met a career civil servant who had just decided to quit. I asked him why, and he said he felt like an ant on a log floating down the river. He felt like he was the ant yelling "go left, go left!" or "go right, go right!"—but of course it didn't make any difference. I could see his point, but I wasn't discouraged from my interest in international security, since I wasn't planning on a career in government.

Meanwhile, every day on the bus to work, I passed the Arlington National Cemetery. Over the course of the summer, I noticed that the grave markers were creeping down the side of the hill, bringing home the reality of the war in Vietnam.

Bureau of the Budget, 1966. After working in the Pentagon, I looked for another opportunity to learn about political–military affairs from the inside. This time, I looked for an organization whose goal was to reduce rather than expand military spending. So I chose the Bureau of the Budget. I found that the military assistance programs other than Vietnam had only two budget officers for roughly a billion dollars. Once there, I chose to scrutinize our large program for the Republic of China (i.e., Taiwan). It seemed to me that Taiwan was arguing that the United States had to provide ever more military assistance, or Taiwan wouldn't be able to protect itself from invasion from the mainland. Fifty years ago, that argument was implausible, so I was motivated to study the Bureau's proposed Taiwan budget for the next five years, and I recommended substantial cuts. I thought my theme would best be illustrated by including a *Peanuts* cartoon showing Lucy saying to Charlie Brown something like, "If you don't tell me you love me I'll hold my breath until I die." I asked if I could include the cartoon in my top-secret report and was told, "Sure, why not?" So I did.

Three years later, I went back and asked about the report I wrote that summer. I was told that in fact it had been useful as added ammunition in cutting back some excessive military aid for Chiang Kai-shek.

RAND, 1967. My next internship was in Santa Monica, California, at the RAND Corporation, then in its heyday as a leading think tank for the Pentagon. I worked for Andy Marshall, who was interested in the role of bureaucratic politics in shaping foreign policy. (Andy went on to become a leading intellectual, a so-called Yoda of the Pentagon, for four decades.) I distinctly remember a hallway discussion that took place between Marshall and the future secretary of defense, another RAND economist, James Schlesinger. Schlesinger in particular argued that war would be with us forever, and I objected (not very forcefully since I was a lowly grad student) that history has seen lots of major changes already, so we shouldn't accept war as inevitable. Looking back on it, I can now say that at least we haven't had a large war between major powers in more than seventy years, so maybe something has changed after all.

Building on my experience analyzing the Military Assistance Program, I spent three weeks in Washington interviewing people in all the relevant organizations to see how they learned lessons from the recent Six-Day War between Israel and most of its neighbors. I found that the lessons learned were very narrow, and the policy positions of the various agencies involved depended not only on the position in a two-dimensional policy space but also on the personal preferences of their leaders. I even got a publication out of it.[3]

When I returned to RAND from my interviews in Washington, I

found that I had forgotten the combination to my top-secret file cabinet. So I went to the security office and told the clerk my room number and she looked up the combination and gave it to me. So I said, "Hey, you just gave me the combination, but you don't know me from Adam." I'll never forget her reply. "Well, most people are honest." I pondered whether to report her to her superior. What would you do? (I decided that the penalty for such an infraction might be too great, so I didn't. But maybe I should have.)

CHAPTER 5

POLITICAL SCIENCE IN GRADUATE SCHOOL

Having decided to pursue a PhD in political science, I was fortunate to be accepted into Yale, which had a terrifically stimulating PhD program in political science. I had many excellent teachers at Yale, including Hayward Alker, Karl Deutsch, and Robert Lane. The professor I most admired was Robert Dahl. His books on local politics and democratic theory taught me that the presentation of research should make the work look easy, although making it look easy took a lot of work.

I hadn't taken any economics in college, but I challenged myself by taking the sequence designed for the PhD students who had been admitted to that very strong program. I hoped it would be sufficient preparation to read Paul Samuelson's undergraduate *Economics* textbook. And I managed to do fine. The most memorable moment came when Professor James Tobin, future Nobel Prize winner, was presenting a formal model of consumer behavior at the blackboard. At one point, a student interrupted to say, "But professor, that's not how people behave." Tobin turned around and said simply, "You're right," and turned back to the board to continue his presentation. To me this was a cogent way to socialize future economists. The point was that we economists know perfectly well that our formal models aren't necessarily good representations of how people behave, and that's okay. It was a powerful lesson for those graduate students in what it meant to be an economist. I was fortunate to figure out early in my graduate career that I preferred political science where the realities of human behavior were taken very seriously. I now see, however, that many economists do care deeply about how people respond to incentives and how their choices lead to large-scale economic outcomes.

In graduate school I resumed my interest in game theory because it used mathematics to address problems of cooperation and conflict. In college I had learned the basics of game theory on my own from an early textbook called *Games and Decisions*.[4] The very first sentence of the book was "in all of man's written record, there has been a preoccupation with conflict of interest; possibly only the topics of God, love, and inner struggle have received comparable attention." As I read the book, I looked for a definition of "conflict of interest," but there was none. I imagined that conflict of interest could be thought of as a matter of degree. The least conflict of interest would occur if the players were in a partnership so that any gains for one player would automatically provide equal gains to the other player. The greatest conflict of interest would be if the players were in a zero-sum game in which gains by one player would automatically result in equal losses for the other. I wondered how to conceptualize this idea in a way that would allow for situations that were somewhere between a partner relationship and a zero-sum game. In graduate school I returned to this problem.

I realized that the ideal way to operationalize the definition of conflict of interest would be one in which there was only one "natural" way to do the measurement. I took as my inspiration the way Claude Shannon had shown that there is one and only one natural way to operationalize the concept of information. He did this by providing a list of properties that a measure of information should have, and he then proved that there was a unique way to measure information in a message that had all of those properties.[5]

My general idea was that the greater the conflict of interest, the greater the likelihood that conflictful behavior would result. I thought that the easiest game to analyze would be a simple bargaining game developed by John Nash who won a Nobel Prize in economics. In the Nash bargaining game there are two players who bargain with each other to try to reach a binding agreement. If their agreement is feasible, then both get what they agreed upon. But if they can't reach a feasible agreement, each gets nothing, and the status quo continues. Nash had proposed that the agreement that the players would reach would be the one that maximized the product of their gains.

I thought that the least conflict of interest would occur if, for example, there was an apple and an orange, and one player only cared about the apple and the other player only cared about the orange. The most conflict of interest would be if they had to agree on how to divide something they both cared about equally, such as a fixed sum of money. In that case, a gain by one would be a loss by the other, assuming agreement could be reached at all. But what would be a good way to measure the amount of conflict of interest for other bargaining situations?

Inspired by Shannon's axiomatic approach to defining a measure of information using a list of properties, I asked myself, "What properties should a measure of conflict of interest have?" I knew, for example, that a measure of conflict of interest should depend on how much better than the status quo a given agreement would be for each player. I also knew the measure should *not* depend on what units were used to measure how much better off a player would be from such an agreement. I also figured the measure should take into account the maximum value that each player could attain from the range of feasible agreements. And I also assumed it should take into account the value each player would receive from the specific agreement that Nash had proposed. But after struggling on and off for two years, I didn't have an answer.

Then, in the summer before my second year in graduate school, I thought about what project I might work on for a research seminar I would be taking in the fall. I thought that my old problem of developing a good measure of conflict of interest would be suitable. Then, one morning, I woke up with the answer. Just like that. I knew it would work: it would satisfy all the properties I wanted, and I was confident I could prove it was the one and only way of measuring conflict of interest in Nash bargaining games that did have all the desired properties.[6] The Nash bargaining game can be analyzed in terms of the demands made by each of the two players. Some pairs of demands are feasible bargains, and some are not. My measure of conflict of interest in such a bargaining game was simply the proportion of all joint demands that are not feasible. This was a pleasing discovery since it was one of those things that are obvious once you say them, but not before.

For my PhD dissertation I needed at least one good example to demonstrate that my measure of conflict of interest could help explain real political events. The example I chose was the formation of parliamentary coalitions. Italy provided the best case because there had been a lot of coalitions, and the order of the eight parties could be specified on a single left–right dimension. My theory was simple: the most likely outcome of the coalition formation process would be a coalition of parties that not only had a working majority of the seats in the parliament but also minimized the conflict of interest among the coalition members. I'll save the report about my testing of this theory for chapter 12 on Minimizing the Strangeness of Bedfellows.

Having been raised to value education, I was fortunate to have been able to attend the outstanding high school in Evanston, Illinois; a college program at the University of Chicago that was well suited to my intellectual bent; and a PhD program in political science at Yale that was arguably the best in the country. I also benefited from a diverse set of six valuable summer internships. It was a splendid education indeed.

PART II

BEING THERE

BEING THERE

CHAPTER 6

BERKELEY IN A TIME OF TROUBLES, 1968–74

As I was finishing my dissertation in 1968, I applied for political science jobs. Luckily for me, it was a time of great demand for new hires, and candidates were in short supply. Having been born in 1943, I was in the "baby trough," so there were relatively few people in my age cohort on the market at the same time as I was. On the demand side, the time I entered the market happened to be just at the peak of when the baby boomers were entering college, so there was a national need to hire more faculty to match the increasing enrollments.

My first job visit was at the University of Chicago. I asked the chair of the department what the salary might be. His reply suggested just how naïve I was in not realizing that in academia, one doesn't ask about starting salaries for tenure-track positions until offered a job. He simply said, "If you are interested in salary you should go to the University of Georgia." It was one of the few times I wished I had kept my curiosity in check.

I was delighted when I was offered a job at the Berkeley campus of the University of California. The department was excellent, the university was world-renowned, and the San Francisco Bay Area had the ideal combination of climate, cuisine, and scenery.

On my very first day of teaching, a student walked in with a pet German shepherd. I didn't know what to do but I decided to say nothing and see how it would go. The student sat in the front row. Once the class began, the German shepherd followed my every move and was as attentive as anyone could ask for.

My teaching was rated as very good, in general, but except for small graduate seminars it was hardly outstanding. I was too low key to generate much excitement when there were more than a few dozen students in the class. I now regret that I never took the trouble to get help to become a better teacher. On the other hand, I think I was a useful mentor to many advanced graduate students and young colleagues.

As I was working to develop a good case for tenure, I asked a very productive sociologist, Seymour Martin Lipset, how he managed to get so much done. He offered this advice, "Don't imagine you'll be less busy six months from now just because you don't know what you'll be busy with." Quite a number of times his advice proved decisive in helping me avoid accepting some seemingly attractive commitment to attend a conference, write a chapter for someone else's edited book, or give a guest lecture. I've developed a corollary that I find helpful, "Avoid a commitment to do something in the future that you wouldn't accept if it needed to be done within two weeks."

Over the years I've offered the "Don't imagine . . ." advice to many colleagues. After a while they usually come back to me with one of two responses. Some thank me for helping them avoid distractions from what they really wanted to get done. Others said that when they are up against a deadline on a project that they shouldn't have committed themselves to, they wish they had followed Lipset's advice.

My first year at Berkeley was marked by three major student protests. The first was a campaign to force the university to establish a Third World College. Then there was a teaching assistants' strike that closed the campus for a week. Finally came a protest march against the university's shutting down the facilities at an empty lot known as People's Park.

The People's Park protest captures a lot about Berkeley in the late 1960s. In February 1968, the university demolished the buildings on a plot of land it owned a few blocks from the main campus. The idea was to build a new dormitory there, but it became clear that the money would not be available for at least three years. The following April, students and local residents decided to turn the vacant lot into a park. They rented a bulldozer for a day or two, but mostly they worked by hand to clear the rubble, grade the area, plant grass, and put in a few benches and swings. The University responded with announcements that *they* owned the land and that they were going to make it into an intramural soccer field.

On May 15, about 4,000 people marched from central campus to reclaim the park for the people. Almost 500 police officers defended the lot, and numerous clashes followed. The day ended with six police officers injured on one side while on the other there were 120 injuries including forty with shotgun wounds. A bystander on the roof of a building overlooking the march was shot and killed when police thought he was making a threatening gesture.

That night, Governor Ronald Reagan issued a proclamation prohibiting loitering at night and any public gathering in the city of Berkeley. There was no need to officially call out the National Guard because the campus was still in a "State of Extreme Emergency" from earlier protests that demanded a Third World College. Soon, there were 2,000 soldiers on the scene.

There were also all sorts of police officers. Some were the local Berkeley city police who were generally friendly and restrained. There were also California Highway Patrol officers who were tough but professional. There were also police from nearby cities including the special riot unit from San Francisco. And then there were the so-called Blue Meanies: Alameda County Sheriff's deputies who had little use for hippies or fine legal distinctions about the use of force.

Further demonstrations, tear gas, and crowd control maneuvers by the National Guard followed for several days, punctuated by a helicopter dispersing tear gas over the entire city. Some of the tear gas used in Berkeley was the kind that causes projectile vomiting.

The university was deeply divided not only by the war in Vietnam but also by a range of cultural and political issues. One year the city council put an extensive list of policy issues on the ballot, ranging from specific proposals within its purview to proposed declarations on a range of national and international issues. While waiting in line to vote, I noticed that standing right in front of me in line was Professor Edward Teller, a right-wing nuclear physicist and later an advocate of the Star Wars missile defense scheme. When we compared notes on our voting intentions,

I was pleased to see that I canceled his vote on every issue, and he was amazed that anyone with a PhD could be so stupid.

The Political Science Department itself was also deeply divided. Some of my colleagues were publicly supporting the Vietnam War, resulting in the need for us to take turns attending their big lectures lest they needed help dealing with angry students. Other colleagues were antiwar, as I was, and a few were not only against the war but also more broadly anti-establishment. I became politically active—a topic I'll leave for the chapter entitled "Getting Out of the Ivory Tower."

I had the usual administrative assignments in the Political Science Department. These were routine, except for one year when I served on the Graduate Admissions Committee. A student from Saudi Arabia applied with a poor undergraduate record, and our committee recommended to the chair that we not admit him to our PhD program. But a professor in the department who specialized in Middle East studies appealed to the chair, telling him that the applicant was a nephew of the king of Saudi Arabia, and it would be a great help to the professor to have him as a student in our department. The chair overruled our recommendation and admitted the applicant. As we expected, the student, Faisal bin Musaid, did poorly and dropped out of the program. No longer a student and apparently with his generous allowance cut off, bin Musaid went back to Saudi Arabia and assassinated the king.

The assassination felt remote, but struggles at Berkeley over student rights, recognition of racial divisions, and the war in Vietnam were all things I saw firsthand—sometimes as an activist and sometimes as an anguished bystander. My own Department of Political Science was deeply divided on all these issues, but I managed to function pretty well. In fact, the department recommended me for tenure ahead of the normal schedule, and I was told in writing by the chair, "You undoubtedly have a brilliant career in this department." But then the College of Literature and the Arts turned me down and told the department never to put me up for tenure again. No reason was given.

What could explain this sudden reversal of fortune? Had I made an enemy of a senior faculty member? Should I have specialized in a single area of research (Latin American politics, for example) instead of working and publishing in several? Was there anything to a secondhand report that my use of math was seen (absurdly) as evidence that I was a threat to the left-wing values of the college Executive Committee?

Not being promoted to tenure meant that I was out. Needless to say, that evoked a good deal of anxiety. Fortunately the University of Michigan had an opening and offered me tenure there. Then, with Michigan's offer on the table, Berkeley relented. I thought about it overnight. I liked California but I was ready for a change.

CHAPTER 7

WALKING THE INTERDISCIPLINARY WALK AT MICHIGAN, 1974–

The offer from Michigan was terrific: it included a tenured joint appointment with political science and a new policy institute that eventually became the Gerald R. Ford School of Public Policy. The faculty at both units were excellent, and at the new policy institute the joint was jumping with activity and enthusiasm. Also attractive was that Michigan had arguably the world's best collection of social science departments and related professional schools. Not only that, but these departments and schools actively encouraged their faculty to collaborate with each other.

I liked the idea of a joint appointment with a policy institute as well as a Political Science Department because my interests were not just in understanding the world but also seeing how I could contribute to making it better. I enjoyed teaching two different kinds of graduate students: the political science doctoral students who wanted to know how to add to our knowledge and the public policy master's students who wanted to know what can be applied in practice.

Berkeley offered climate, cuisine, and scenery, but I decided that Michigan was a better place for my work, and I knew I'd kick myself in ten years if I didn't accept their offer.

In retrospect, my least creative period was the six years at Berkeley when I was trying to please others by building what I hoped would be a good case for tenure.

My closest friend and colleague at Michigan was Michael Cohen. Like me, he was a political scientist with an interest in public policy. Like me, too, he was a math modeler who enjoyed doing computer simulations of social processes. His main interest was in organization theory, which nicely complemented my interest in international affairs. I have had to work hard at being modest and self-effacing but to Michael it came naturally.

When Michael was interviewed by Elinor Ostrom for a biographical essay about me, what he said about me could apply just as well to him:

> The research I have done without him bears his influence almost as much as the dozen or so pieces we have co-authored. [He] is an exceedingly forthright research partner. When an idea or a draft won't stand up, he says so calmly, but firmly—and he always has solid reasons. If you can muster even more compelling arguments in response, he will readily accept them. But he won't concede until you and he have converged on an air-tight analysis.[1]

When we met in 1974, Michael was already established as an influential organizational theorist, being the lead author of a famous article with the amusing title of "A Garbage Can Model of Organizational Choice."[2] The idea was that just as a garbage can might contain almost any content, an opportunity for an organizational choice might become the arena for contesting almost any issue, whether or not it was related to the issue at hand.

We wound up collaborating on nine articles and a book. The book was intended to show how complexity theory, with its emphasis on adaptive systems, could help explain how organizations work and provide insights into how organizations might be designed to work better. We had no trouble coming up with the subtitle: *Organizational Implications of a Scientific Frontier*. But I distinctly remember our struggles to come up with a good title. After much back and forth, we finally came up with something that was obvious only in retrospect: *Harnessing Complexity*.[3] The only disagreement we ever had concerned who would be the first author. Michael eventually deferred to my preference on the grounds that I was better known and the book might therefore get more attention if I were the first author—but, looking back, I realize that I should have agreed to his being the first author because the book was about how organizations work, and that was his field, not mine.

Michael introduced me to a delightful character: John Holland. John received the world's first PhD in computer science. He had a magically infectious smile, a childlike curiosity, and the ability to make any research project seem like pure fun. The three of us decided to meet regularly to share our mutual interests centered on using agent-based models to simulate all sorts of complex adaptive systems from microbes to nations. John then recruited a former teacher of his, Art Burks. Art had worked with John von Neumann on the earliest computers. We named our group BACH for the initials of its founding members: Burks, Axelrod, Cohen, and Holland. Rick Riolo, a computer scientist, was also a member from the start.

The roster of the BACH group over the years was very impressive. One of the twentieth century's leading evolutionary biologists, William Hamilton, was a member of BACH from about 1979 until he left to return to England in 1984 for his appointment as the Royal Society research professor in the Department of Zoology at Oxford; mathematician/economist Carl Simon became a member around 1982. When we recruited Doug Hofstadter, author of the Pulitzer Prize–winning book *Gödel, Escher, Bach* and a *Scientific American* columnist to came to Michigan in 1984, we immediately invited him to join the BACH group. He and his student Melanie Mitchell enriched the workshops with a new interest in using computer models to explore the essence of analogical thinking. Hofstadter returned to Indiana University in 1988, and microbiologist Michael Savageau was invited to the table, especially as the group became more interested in biological analogies to computer-based problem solving. Later members included Scott Page, an outstanding political scientist who modeled diversity in institutions; Mark Newman, a physicist who did pioneering work in the theory of networks; and Mercedes Pascual, an ecologist who studied population dynamics and the spread of disease.

Starting in 1975 or 1976, the BACH group met almost every other week for two hours of intense discussion. The group had amazing longevity: it was sustained without a break for more than twenty-five years. John Holland was the convener and helped establish the norms of friendly criticism and playful work. Our sessions were usually devoted to one of us presenting our current ideas and problems. Doing this in rough rotation meant that we'd each have a chance to get help every couple of months. Since we came to know each other's work very well, we didn't have to censor our thoughts or worry about appearing idiotic. Moreover, we were able to pick up where we had left off each time. Whether I was presenting my own half-baked ideas or trying to help others develop theirs, the experience always made me feel energized and perhaps a bit smarter than I was when I walked into the room.

In the BACH group we were all enabled to look foolish. The value of being able to look foolish is that you can then allow yourself to be creative. You can try out off-the-wall ideas, most of which are bound to look (and be) silly. Of course, in almost all settings there is a real cost to looking foolish. But an important exception is that there is almost no cost in looking foolish with people who know you so well that their assessment of you will not be significantly lowered by hearing some stupid ideas.

So I've come to value friends and colleagues who know me so well that I can be comfortable that their estimation of my intelligence won't suffer too much from some evidence that I'm really not as smart as they might have thought.

A corollary of the principle that it pays to find settings in which you can look foolish is that it pays to hang around really smart people. Sure, there are many reasons to hang around really smart people, including that they are generally very interesting, you can learn a lot from them, and they are capable of giving you useful feedback on your own ideas. Really smart people can tell you things worth hearing about, including things you'd never heard of before or thought much about. Engaging with them can help you think more clearly and deeply. But an additional reason is that really smart people who know you well are in a good position to help you distinguish which ideas of yours are worth pursuing, and which might not be. And they might well be in a good position to help you think about what to read or try next.

I've made a habit of traveling to visit friends with whom I can look foolish, typically for two or three days. This is long enough to have time to waste by allowing our conversation to wander in unexpected directions. Four people I've visited in this way for over thirty years are Steve Crocker (a computer scientist), Bob Putnam (a political scientist), Steph

Figure 2. The BACH group in the late 1980s, from left to right: Michael Cohen, Robert Axelrod, William Hamilton, Arthur Burks, John Holland, Rick Riolo, Michael Savageau, and Carl Simon.

anie Forrest (another computer scientist), and Dave Axelrod (my brother, a geneticist). More recently I've added Scott Atran (an anthropologist), Ken Pienta (an oncologist), and Doug Hofstadter (a cognitive scientist and writer). In these visits, we typically take turns describing our current and future interests, as well as offering deep, incisive, no-holds-barred but affectionate criticism of one another's ideas.

The central theme of the BACH group was complexity, especially complex systems that adapted to their environment. John Holland led the way with his invention of an algorithm that was inspired by evolutionary biology. It used biologically inspired operations such as mutation, crossover, and selection to simulate an evolving population. The technique proved very effective for generating high-quality solutions to a wide class of problems such as optimization and search, with applications in engineering, biology, computer science, economics, and many other fields.

In the BACH group, much of our work was based on the use of evolutionary thinking to explore social science issues in terms of a population of actors. What we were doing was very different from the traditional equation-based modeling exemplified in many economic models of rational actors. Instead, we explored situations in which the actors were adaptive rather than rational. We also found that when the interactions between the actors involved contingencies and nonlinear effects, solving equations via deductive methods was simply not possible, but simulations of artificial histories could provide insights. Put another way, we were using agent-based modeling rather than equation-based modeling.

In high school I had developed a primitive form of an agent-based model with my hypothetical organisms and environments. But I had simulated actors one at a time rather than allowing them to interact. The BACH group helped me to appreciate the capacity of agent-based modeling to gain insights into a variety of complex adaptive systems. I've been using agent-based modeling ever since. I've been pleased to see that agent-based modeling has been catching on in the social sciences: one indication is the number of times an online guide for newcomers has been downloaded since Leigh Tesfatsion and I posted the first version in 2005. By 2022, the guide had been downloaded more than 180,000 times.[4]

The BACH group had strong connections with Santa Fe Institute in New Mexico. I benefited from five or six visits. The institute attracted researchers from many disciplines to work on problems related to the theme of complexity. But getting them to benefit from each other's presence wasn't easy. For example, when physicists and biologists convene to discuss dynamical systems, they often trip over the question of whether the dynamics move up or down in abstract space. I distinctly remember one such incident when I was able to forestall what was becoming a heated debate by pointing out that they were really talking about two different things: the physicists were thinking about potential energy, which tends to go down in accordance with the second law of thermodynamics, and the biologists were thinking about fitness, which tends to go up according to Darwin's theory of evolution. With my interdisciplinary perspective, I was able to explain to each side how they were really talking about two ways of viewing the same thing, namely adaptation to the environment.

While I had done a lot of interdisciplinary work, my own home turf was political science. I was deeply appreciative in 2006 when I was elected president of the American Political Science Association. A perk of the office is that one's intellectual biography is published as an essay in one of the association's journals. I asked Lin Ostrom if she would be willing to write mine, and she graciously agreed. Little did I know that three years later she would be awarded the Nobel Prize in economics, becoming the only political scientist ever to be so honored. Reading what she wrote was an opportunity for me to see myself through someone else's eyes. This was my favorite part:

> His fascination and distress about threats to peace is a major source of the fantastic energy he has brought to his work. Simultaneously, his insistence on rigorous exploration on the processes that enhance cooperation in complex settings has ensured that his theoretical breakthroughs have been widely recognized across the social sciences as well as in biology and computer sciences.[5]

As president of the American Political Science Association, I did my best to promote interdisciplinary work. My presidential speech was about how political science can contribute to other disciplines.[6] I was also able to raise money from the National Science Foundation for a study of the role of interdisciplinary work in the context of a discipline-based academy. To that end, John Aldrich did a fine job of recruiting people to write impressive chapters for an edited volume.[7]

But enough about the context of my interdisciplinary activity. Let's turn now to the work itself.

PART III

COOPERATION

CHAPTER 8

TOURNAMENTS

I learned about game theory as an undergraduate from a book recommended by a friend: *Games and Decisions* by Duncan Luce and Howard Raiffa.[1] The book explained that game theory was the study of how rational players should make choices when the outcome depended not only on their own choice but also on others' choices. As I mentioned earlier, I was intrigued by the book's opening sentence about the ubiquity of "conflict of interest," a term that the book never defined. This led me to do my PhD dissertation using game theory to develop and test predictions about how conflicts of interest affect political behaviors such as coalition formation.

The same book introduced me to the Prisoner's Dilemma, a game between two players that captures the essence of a fundamental problem: namely, the tension between doing what is good for the individual (a selfish choice called a defection) and what is good for both (a cooperative choice). Both players can do well if both cooperate. But each player has an incentive to defect, because defection has a higher payoff *no matter* what the other player chooses.[2] An example of a Prisoner's Dilemma is an arms race in which each side races ahead for fear of being at a disadvantage, but both sides would have been better off if they had slowed down or stopped their arms race. Luce and Raiffa pointed out that rational players, knowing that defection was better no matter what the other did, would then both defect. They also pointed out that if the game were played twice, rational players would surely defect on the second move, just as they would in the single-play game. But if they would both defect

45

on the second move, rational players would then also defect on the first move because there was no reason not to. Luce and Raiffa then pointed out that this logic would lead rational players to defect on each move of a three-move game, a four-move game, and, indeed, a repeated Prisoner's Dilemma of any length, as long as the players knew in advance how long the game would last. The reasoning was that defection would be the dominant strategy on the last move, and therefore on the next-to-last move as well, and so on all the way back to the first move.

The logic was impeccable, but I was skeptical that this logic captured how people behave in the real world. It seemed to me that if I were playing with a real person who understood the game, I would not expect the other person to perform a backwards induction for (say) 200 moves, and the other person probably wouldn't expect me to, either—even if we both understood the Prisoner's Dilemma, and even if we both understood that the other understood it. Instead, I imagined that I would at least try some cooperation at the beginning just to see if we couldn't get something going. That led me to wonder how one *should* play the game, knowing that the other might also be looking for a way out of never-ending mutual defection. The question for me then became "how should a sophisticated player act when players are each trying to maximize their own payoff independent of what the other player gains?"

Looking back, I see that my interest in finding out how sophisticated individuals would play to maximize their own score was a means to an end. What I really wanted to know was how to *promote* cooperation. While I could not have articulated it at the time, I can now offer a rendition of the intuition I had at the time. Wanting to know how to promote cooperation, I saw the iterated Prisoner's Dilemma as an excellent testbed. I wasn't satisfied with the results of lab experiments with college students who had just been introduced to the game, just as I wouldn't have been satisfied with understanding how experienced people play chess by simply watching beginners. So I looked at the game theory literature in search of strategies that had been advocated by experts. I was intrigued to find a number of quite different strategies based on concepts like Bayesian learning, reciprocity, dynamic programming, and deterrence.

In fact, the literature on the iterated Prisoner's Dilemma provided no clear answer to the question of how to avoid conflict, or even how an individual (or country) should play the game on their own behalf. I knew from published lab experiments that people did not play a consistent strategy but would instead employ a lot of trial and error, sometimes just out of boredom. I also expected that trying to analyze such behavior to determine what made for success would be very hard. I explored letting someone interact with a computer program that used a specific strategy that was known to me but not known to the player. I tried this out on a world-class social scientist, James March, who was already familiar with the iterated Prisoner's Dilemma. I was dismayed when he took delight in the fact that, after a few moves, he was doing better than the computer— without realizing that *both* were doing poorly. That's when I realized that to observe and analyze sophisticated players I would need both sides to play carefully designed strategies that would cover all contingencies.

My next step was to take the variety of published strategies that had been proposed in the literature and program a computer to see what would happen if two of these strategies met each other. From there, it was only a small step to invite others to submit strategies that they designed to do well for themselves knowing that they would be interacting with other strategies that were also designed to do well for *themselves*.

Practitioners as well as students and scholars have frequently asked me, "How did you get the idea in the first place to run a computer tournament for the Prisoner's Dilemma?" The short answer is that the computer tournament combined two of my long-standing interests: artificial intelligence and game theory. As mentioned earlier, I was exposed to artificial intelligence at my summer job at Northwestern University's Computer Center when I came across a just-published article by Arthur Samuel that described a checkers-playing program that learned to improve its own play and was then able to beat its creator.[3] Afterwards, I followed the development of computer chess through the 1960s as well as the computer chess tournaments that began in 1970. In the late 1970s, when I wanted to identify a good strategy for playing the iterated Prisoner's Dilemma, the idea of a computer tournament came readily to mind.

I invited professional game theorists to send in entries in the form of a computer program that would encode their favorite strategy to play the iterated Prisoner's Dilemma. Each program was an algorithm that would, at each move, have the history of the game for input and have a choice of either cooperate or defect as output. As announced in the rules of the tournament, each entry would be paired with each other entry, with its own twin, and with a completely random strategy. Since the participants knew that they were being recruited primarily from a pool of those who were familiar with the Prisoner's Dilemma they could be assured that their own strategy would be facing rules of play designed by other informed participants. Such recruitment would also guarantee that the state of the art was represented in the tournament. I received fourteen entries from five disciplines: political science, economics, psychology, sociology, and mathematics. I was quite pleased that the tournament allowed people from different disciplines to interact on a common task.

The winning strategy was TIT FOR TAT submitted by Anatol Rapoport of the University of Toronto, a well-known peace researcher. TIT FOR TAT is the strategy of cooperating on the first move and then doing whatever the other player did on the previous move. I was amazed that the most effective strategy was the simplest of all those submitted. Based on the literature about computer chess tournaments, I had originally thought that the most effective strategy for the iterated Prisoner's Dilemma would probably be quite complex. But the exact opposite turned out to be the case. I found that the very simple reciprocity of TIT FOR TAT tended to evoke cooperation from a wide range of *other* strategies and therefore did well for *itself*.

The effectiveness of a given strategy depends not only on its own characteristics but also on the nature of the other strategies it will interact with. For this reason, the results of a single tournament are not definitive. So I organized a second round of the tournament for the iterated Prisoner's Dilemma. This time, I recruited contestants though announcements in computer hobbyist magazines as well as the professionals who submitted entries in the first round. Potential entrants were told about the results of the first round, the concepts I had used to analyze what worked well, and the strategic pitfalls that I had discovered. This meant that the second round could begin at a higher level of sophistication than the first round. This time, there were sixty-three entries including the random strategy. The contestants ranged from a ten-year-old computer hobbyist to professors of computer science and evolutionary biology in addition to individuals from five disciplines represented in the first round.

When I ran the new tournament and saw the results, I was taken aback. "Again?" I asked myself. Yes, TIT FOR TAT won the second round too, even though everyone knew it was the strategy to beat. And it won even though it was the simplest strategy in both tournaments. I was amazed. But I was also delighted. I immediately realized that there was something going on here that was really worth exploring and trying to understand. It was the most exciting moment in my career.

In analyzing the millions of choices in the tournaments, I was surprised to find that—although TIT FOR TAT won both rounds of the tournament—it never once did better than any of the wide range of strategies it interacted with. In fact, I came to realize that it *couldn't* do better than the player it was interacting with. The reason is that to do better than the player you are interacting with, you have to defect more than the other side does. And TIT FOR TAT never does that. It starts with cooperation and never defects unless the other player has just defected. So it can't defect more times than the other player and therefore can't do better than the other player. But it won both rounds of the tournament, outperforming every other strategy! TIT FOR TAT was effective because it elicited more cooperation from other players than any other strategy. Or, as one reviewer said, "Nice guys finish first." This can't happen in a zero-sum game like chess or football, but it can and did happen in the iterated Prisoner's Dilemma.

To understand how the simple reciprocity of TIT FOR TAT managed to elicit so much cooperation from others I started with the raw data of the three million choices generated in the tournament. I cheerfully took up the challenge of making sense of it all. The first major finding was that the rules that were never the first to defect tended to score very well. So it paid not to start trouble. I couldn't find a good word for this property, so I called these entries "nice." My second major finding was that a property that distinguished TIT FOR TAT from many other entries was that it was forgiving: if the other player cooperated after a defection, TIT FOR TAT immediately went from echoing the defection to cooperating again when the other player did. The third property was somewhat surprising to me: it paid to be provoked by even one defection from the other player. I had anticipated that it would be better to be somewhat patient when the other player started defecting, but I was wrong. It paid to respond promptly. In sum, TIT FOR TAT's effectiveness in eliciting cooperation from the other player and thereby doing well for itself was based on its being nice, forgiving, and provokable.

Wanting to see just how robust was the success of TIT FOR TAT, I asked myself a series of questions.

- What would happen in a world where almost all the players were pure defectors? To answer this, I proved with a little algebra that even a small cluster of TIT FOR TAT players can invade and take over a population of pure defectors.
- Did TIT FOR TAT eat its own lunch? In other words, was TIT FOR TAT's success simply due to its exploiting weak rules that might not be around in the future? To check this possibility, I ran of series of simulations in which weak players tended to drop out of the population. The result was that TIT FOR TAT still did better than any of the other submissions.
- Was TIT FOR TAT's success dependent on the particular rules of the tournaments, or could it evolve from a completely random initial population? Working with Stephanie Forrest, my research assistant at the time and now a distinguished professor at Arizona State University, I used John Holland's genetic algorithm to do an evolutionary simulation.[4] The results are quite remarkable: from a strictly random start, the genetic algorithm evolved populations whose median member was just as successful as the best rule in the tournament, TIT FOR TAT. Most of the strategies that evolved in the simulation actually resembled TIT FOR TAT, having many of the properties that make TIT FOR TAT so successful, including forgiveness and provokability.
- Some critics asked what would happen if there were some noise or misunderstanding in the interactions between the players. The answer was that adding a little generosity or contrition to TIT FOR TAT's pure reciprocity was sufficient to retain its success. I'll explain this later when addressing this and other criticisms.

With the robust success of TIT FOR TAT, I began to see the world as a series of nails waiting for my hammer. Given my interest in evolution-

ary biology and the very simplicity of the Prisoner's Dilemma, I felt that
there might be some useful connections to be made there. Although I
am a political scientist by training, I have long been interested in evolutionary theory. But when I wanted to do research about the evolutionary implications of my work, I knew I was in over my head. So I reached
out to Richard Dawkins, the evolutionary biologist who had entered the
tournament. I asked if he would be interested in collaborating with me.
He suggested that the right person to ask was William Hamilton, who,
unbeknownst to me, happened to be where I was: at the University of
Michigan. I knew of Hamilton's important analysis of what he called
"inclusive fitness,"[5] cooperation based on kinship, an idea developed by
Richard Dawkins in his book *The Selfish Gene*.[6]

So I gave Bill a call.

CHAPTER 9

EVOLUTION

In his memoirs, Bill describes his reactions to my phone call.[7]

> One day in the Museum of Zoology at Ann Arbor there came a phone call from a stranger asking what I knew about evolutionarily stable strategies and for some guidance to relevant literature. Now on the phone to me was someone out of political science who seemed to have just the sort of idea I needed. A live games theorist was here on my own campus! Nervously, and rather the way a naturalist might hope to see his first mountain lion in the woods, I had long yearned for and dreaded an encounter with a games theorist. How did they think? What were their dens full of? Axelrod on the phone sounded nice and, very surprising to me, he was more than a bit biological in his manner of thinking. I sensed at once a possibility that the real games theorists might be going to turn out to be a kind of kindred to us [biologists].[8]

Had Bill known of my long-standing interest in evolutionary theory, he might not have been quite so surprised that my thinking was more than a bit biological. As mentioned earlier, in high school, I wrote a computer simulation to study hypothetical life forms and environments, and in college, my early interest in evolution was nurtured by a summer at the University of Chicago's Committee on Mathematical Biology.

That first phone call led to a lunch. Here is how Bill recalls what happened next:

Soon after the lunch again I proposed that the work seemed so interesting biologically we might try writing it up for a joint paper in *Science*; [Axelrod's] contribution would be the basic ideas plus the description of his tournaments and mine to add a natural scientist's style and some biological illustrations.

I was delighted to accept Bill's invitation to collaborate. Despite our different disciplines, Bill and I shared not only mathematical training but also a love of formal modeling. Bill had even published one paper using the Prisoner's Dilemma, although he had been hoping to get away from that when I dragged him back.

Bill's proposed division of labor turned out to be a good description of how the collaboration developed. I gradually realized, however, just how much was included in Bill's modest formulation of adding "a natural scientist's style and some biological illustrations." Bill's naturalist's style included having at his fingertips an astonishing knowledge of species from bacteria to primates. His experience as a naturalist often gave him the capacity to check out the plausibility of an idea with pertinent examples right off the top of his head. It also helped him to generate surprising new ideas. Here is how Bill saw us working together:

That brilliant cartoonist of the journal *American Scientist*, Sidney Harris, has a picture where a mathematician covers the blackboard with an outpouring of his formal demonstration. It starts top left on the blackboard and ends bottom right with a triumphant "QED." Halfway down, though, one sees a gap in the stream where is written in plain English: "Then a miracle occurs," after which the mathematical argument goes on. Chalk still in his hand, the author of this quod est demonstrandum now stands back and watches with a cold dislike an elderly mathematician who peers at the words in the gap and says: "But I think you need to be a bit more explicit—here in step two." I easily imagine myself to be that enthusiast with the chalk and I also think of many castings for the elderly critic. Yet how easy it is to imagine a third figure—Bob—in the background of the picture, saying cheerfully: "But maybe he has something all the same, maybe that piece can be fixed up. What if . . ."

I shared Bill's surprise at how well we worked together. As he put it:

I would have thought it a leg-pull at the time if someone had told me of a future when I would find it more rewarding to talk "patterns" to political scientists rather than to fellow biologists. Perhaps the most important thing we shared was our aesthetic sense. An intuitive understanding between us was immediate. Both of us always liked to be always understanding new things and to be listening more than talking; both of us had little inclination for the social manoeuvring, all the "who should bow-lowest" stuff, which so often wastes time and adrenalin as new social intercourse starts. Bob is the more logical, but beyond this what we certainly share strongly is a sense for a hard-to-define aesthetic grace that may lurk in a proposition, that which makes one want to believe it before any proof and in the midst a confusion and even antagonism of details. Such grace in an idea seems often to mean that it is right. Rather as I have a quasi-professional artist as my maternal grandmother, Bob has one closer to him—his father. Such forebears perhaps give to both of us the streak that judges claims not in isolation but rather by the shapes that may come to be formed from their interlock, rather as brush strokes in a painting, shapeless or even misplaced considered individually, are overlooked as they join to create a whole.

I see a further connection between art and modeling. My father painted to express how he saw the world, highlighting what was important to him by leaving out what was not. Likewise, my modeling incorporates what is important to my perspective on a problem and leaves out what is not.

Bill's disciplinary training as an evolutionary biologist and a naturalist proved essential to making our theoretical findings compelling to biologists. He was adept at identifying pertinent biological examples so that biologists could see what we were talking about. While not all of his proposed applications have been borne out in subsequent research, he was able to demonstrate the potential relevance of computer tournaments for the major biological puzzle of why individuals cooperate with unrelated others. He was also able to explain what our contribution added to what was already understood about evolution. Specifically, he showed how our modeling provided a solid foundation for many of the insights about altruism formulated years earlier by Robert Trivers. Bill was also able to show how our model could be used by other evolutionary biologists to formulate and test new hypotheses about animal behavior, as well as exploring dozens of variants of the simple iterated Prisoner's Dilemma.

When Hamilton sent Robert Trivers a copy of our paper, Trivers wrote back, saying, "my heart soared." Trivers later wrote that, "For one wild moment, I kidded [Bill], I actually believed there was progress in science!"[9]

Our differing disciplinary backgrounds would show up in surprising ways, as when I visited him in his native Oxford and joined him on a day trip to William Shakespeare's grave. I pondered the psychological question of why Shakespeare might have wanted others to read a simple poem on his gravestone, and Bill pondered the biological puzzle of why a very rare plant was growing on a nearby fence.

Between us and with surprisingly little difficulty we pushed our paper into *Science*.[10] Once published it won the Newcomb-Cleveland Prize as *Science*'s supposed best paper of the year.

Since we worked so well together, I told Bill that if he ever had an idea he'd like to share with me, I would be more than willing to work with him again. Sure enough, several years after he returned to Oxford, he told me that he had an idea about the origin of sexual reproduction. I'll leave that story for later, since I want to get back to what happened after the Prisoner's Dilemma tournament results were published.

CHAPTER 10

TRENCH WARFARE

The habit I started in junior high school of scanning a wide range of journals paid off handsomely when twenty years later I came across a book review in a sociology journal. The book being reviewed was based on the diaries and memoirs of British and German soldiers facing each other in the trench warfare of World War I.[11] These soldiers often employed what they called the "live and let live system." The idea was that, in the lull between large battles ordered by the higher-ups, each side largely refrained from actions that would harm the other side—but only as long as the other side reciprocated such restraint. When I read that book, I realized how it provided a striking example of how opposing military units facing each other for an extended period of time could use what amounted to a TIT FOR TAT strategy to sustain cooperation even in the midst of a brutal war.

I thought of the trench warfare example as a good way to illustrate what I was talking about. I didn't expect it would have much value for convincing people that I was on to something. After all, the trench warfare case was a historical event that I picked out of a huge number of possible historical events. But as it turned out, the trench warfare example was, for many readers, compelling evidence that my research on cooperation was indeed relevant to the real world.

Once I had come across the book on the live and let live system in trench warfare, I thought that I might be able to write a book for an audience that would reach beyond that of my strictly academic publications. I tried out presenting the basic ideas including the trench warfare example to some nonacademics, including my mother-in-law. The uniformly favorable response convinced me that explaining my work to a broad audience was not only possible but had a good chance of being well received.

But frankly, I hate to write. When I do write, I keep thinking of Mao Zedong's saying that making a revolution is like the experience of an arthritic person weaving a basket: you know you can do it, but every step is painful. It's one thing to write one article at a time and quite another to write a book, especially a book that had to be engaging as well as precise.

I discussed the possibility with my good friend Michael Cohen. I told him I was conflicted about taking the time and making the effort to write such a book, as it would take me away from my primary passion: my research. He persuaded me that if I did write the book, then I would, over the course of my career, actually have *more* time to do research. I wasn't sure, but I did think it was worth trying.

As I expected, the writing was hard. Fortunately, my wife, Amy Saldinger, is a terrific editor: critical when necessary and helpful always. She didn't make the act of writing easier, but she did make the final product a lot more accessible and more inviting to read.

When I had a rough draft, I sent it to Doug Hofstadter, who wrote a monthly column called "Metamagical Themas" that I much admired in *Scientific American*. I didn't know him yet, but I thought it was worth a try. He was enthusiastic and did two very helpful things. He wrote a column about the forthcoming book, thereby creating a potential readership. And he introduced me to his own publisher, Martin Kessler of Basic Books. Doug had substantial clout with Mr. Kessler because Doug's *Gödel, Escher, Bach* had won the Pulitzer Prize. Mr. Kessler accepted my book for publication and gave me some useful advice, including, "Every equation halves the number of readers, but it is okay to have technical material in appendices, and doing that could even increase the credibility of the book." He also explained how the table of contents should itself tell a story. When it came time to publish *The Evolution of Cooperation*, Basic Books gave it a marketing boost that no academic press would likely provide. The result was a good deal of media attention including a review in the *New York Times*.

CHAPTER 11

RESPONSES

The reviews were generally quite positive. Although there were some criticisms that I will discuss later, the published reviews were all that I could have hoped for. I also got a good deal of fan mail. My favorite was from a correspondent who said he was "seat-edged" while reading it.

Publishers in other countries chose to translate the book, eventually making it available in twelve languages. One of the first translations was to Swedish, which puzzled me, since potential readers in Sweden would very likely be able to read the original. I was especially pleased by the publication in Arabic, not only because I hoped people in the Middle East and North Africa would read it but also because surprisingly few books were translated into Arabic; in fact, the Arab Human Development Report said in 2002 that "the number of books translated into Arabic yearly is no more than 330, or one-fifth of those translated in a small country like Greece."

Perhaps the most gratifying response was election by my fellow scientists to the National Academy of Sciences in 1986. I was the youngest political scientist to be so chosen.

The next year came a MacArthur Fellowship. What can one say about receiving *that* news? Well, there is someone who described the experience better than I can: Denise Shekerjian, who interviewed a number of winners for her study of creativity. She starts her book as follows.[12]

This project was born from a line in the newspaper. "Think of it," was the tease. "You're at home minding your own business when the phone rings. 'You don't know me,' a voice says, 'but I'm calling to congratulate you. In recognition and encouragement of your creative capabilities, you have just been awarded a prize in the six-figure range to be paid out over the next five years with absolutely no strings attached.'"

I read on. The facts were staggering. Anywhere from thirty to seventy thousand dollars a year for five years. . . . No applications allowed. No follow-up or accountability of any kind. Top-drawer prestige. A steady stream of checks in the mailbox. Cash them, or bank them, or rip them up in a sorry moment of madness—the decision entirely yours, no explanations sought nor owed.

In the beginning it was the fairy-tale freedom that attracted me to the MacArthur Award. Win a MacArthur and enjoy the ease of financial strain, the gift of time, and the star-making machinery that goes along with it all.

As Shekerjian said, there is no accountability of any kind. In my case, I used the fellowship primarily to buy release time from teaching.

As I contemplate the fellowship's impact, I realize that it was almost impossible to separate it from other honors that I received at about the same time. In 1985, I was elected to the American Academy of Arts and Science; in 1986, I was elected to the National Academy of Sciences, and then, in 1987, I received the MacArthur Fellowship. These honors, and other recognition of my research on cooperation, transformed how I thought about myself, as well as how others thought about me.

One effect of this transformation was to raise my standards for my own research. I came to feel that I should not be devoting substantial time to projects with good chances of average payoffs. Instead, I felt I should be searching for projects that had some real chance of an extremely large payoff. This conclusion was in part the result of deciding that most work (by myself and others) makes only a modest contribution, but a highly successful program of work can be hundreds of times more valuable than routine work. So I came to see my own research in terms of prospecting for a really promising approach to some important problem.

Over the five years of the fellowship, the search for a project with the potential to make a truly outstanding contribution often led me to a sense of paralysis. Perhaps this sense of paralysis was a result of competition with my own past success. Perhaps it was a part of a normal mid-life crisis in my late forties. Or perhaps it was a consequence of a healthy desire to not be satisfied with merely repeating myself.

Fortunately, the sense of competing with myself gradually faded.

Another effect of the fellowship and other honors is that people listened to me more attentively than they used to. The public attention faded over time, but the credibility lingered. Fortunately, my good friends and anonymous reviewers still tell me when I'm saying something silly.

As a result of my research on cooperation, I received many offers to speak about how to apply my findings in business, education, and government. In responding to these requests I kept in mind Lipset's advice never to imagine you'll be less busy in six months than you are now even though you may not know what you'll be busy with. Some of these opportunities came with a financial incentive. Some were things I really wanted to do, but others seemed like a burden. For those that had less intrinsic appeal, I developed the strategy of figuring out how much money it would take to make me happy to do it. I would then name that figure. If it was accepted, I would indeed be happy to accept the offer, and if it was not accepted, I would be happy not to have to do it.

The only effect I could trace solely to the MacArthur Fellowship is that it gave me "internal permission" to accept membership on the National Academy of Sciences' Committee on International Peace and Security (CISAC). I will discuss this fascinating experience later in the context of getting out of the ivory tower. But let me note here that CISAC was a committee of senior scientists, mostly physicists, who explored the future of arms control with other scientists, chiefly with Soviets and their Russian successors. Before receiving the fellowship, I had been invited to join CISAC, but felt that I did not have the time to devote to its intensive activities, which involved a great deal of travel. However, after receiving the fellowship I was asked again, and this time I decided that with the time that the fellowship would buy for my research, I could devote the necessary time to CISAC without feeling that my research would have to suffer too much.

The anticipation of having more time for my research has also made me feel less conflicted than I would otherwise have been about spending lots of time with Amy and my two daughters, both of whom were born during the period of the fellowship.

As my work was becoming widely known, I began to hear stories of how others applied it in a range of contexts far beyond what I had imagined. Some applications were conveyed to me anecdotally, in cases where my work had inspired personal actions. One professor sought me out at a political science convention to thank me for writing my book. She said it really helped her when her marriage began to crumble.

"Oh, did it save your marriage?," I asked.

"No. I didn't want to save my marriage. But it sure did help with my divorce. I realized that I had let myself be a sucker over and over again in the marriage. I started to play TIT FOR TAT, and once my partner learned that I couldn't be pushed around, I got a much better deal."

Another application was quite creative. A veteran told me that when he was an infantry officer in Iraq, he implemented the idea that one shouldn't be the first to defect. Upon approaching a village that might or might not have been friendly, and even if friendly might well have thought his troops meant them harm, he instructed his soldiers to put their rifles behind their necks as they approached. This served as a clear demonstration that his troops didn't intend to be the first to open fire. And it worked: what could easily have turned into a violent confrontation was resolved peacefully.

Other applications of my work fell within the realm of academic research. In international relations, the evidence is strong that reciprocity is widely employed.[13] For example, Paul Huth showed that reciprocity helps prevent an escalation of interactional crises. He identified fifty-eight cases from 1885 to 1983 of attempted deterrence against an immediate threat, and he categorized them according to whether the defender responded to military actions by the potential attacker with greater, equal, or lesser levels of military preparedness. He found that "a tit for tat policy by the defender increased by 33% the probability of successful deterrence as compared to failing to match or exceeding the military escalation of the potential attacker."[14]

Since it was the Cuban Missile Crisis that helped motivate my decision to pursue political science, I was gratified in 1990 when the

National Academy of Sciences rewarded my work on cooperation with the inaugural prize for Behavioral Research Relevant to the Prevention of Nuclear War.

In biology, there is a growing body of evidence of reciprocity in animals as diverse as birds,[15] vampire bats,[16] and monkeys.[17] My favorite application is an experiment with fish. Asking whether stickleback fish reciprocate cooperation, Manfred Milinski devised a very clever experimental design. When sticklebacks notice a pike, their predator, in the vicinity of the sticklebacks' feeding grounds, they approach the pike gingerly (up to a respectful distance) and take a good look at it.[18] This is called predator inspection and provides the fish with some clues about the current motivation of the pike, and therefore the risk to the sticklebacks if they enter their feeding grounds. This risk, however, is considerably reduced if the sticklebacks approach in pairs, as they frequently do. The danger is reduced by more than half because the efficiency of a predator drops drastically whenever two targets compete for its attention. As long as the two sticklebacks approach together or take the lead in turn, one can speak of cooperation. But if one of them consistently hangs back and gains its information about the pike by waiting in the wings while the other stickleback assumes all of the risk in approaching the pike, this is a clear case of defection. Milinski had a single stickleback confronted with a dummy pike and used a mirror to make the stickleback think that it had a companion. Depending on the position of the mirror, the fake companion either kept abreast or stayed a couple of inches behind. In the former case, the deluded stickleback usually dared to move a bit closer to the pike—a strong hint of a strategy based on reciprocity.

When I saw a research article on infectious disease that seemed to apply my work to viruses and bacteria,[19] I wrote the author, Dr. Adin Ross-Gillespie of the University of Zurich, to ask whether his research had been influenced by mine. He replied, "Yes, of course your work has had an influence on ours! Your seminal work attracted many people to the field and helped to demonstrate how the evolutionary study of cooperation has relevance to many disciplines—including, as we argue, the design of strategies to control infectious diseases."

In the realm of human neurobiology, advances are opening new possibilities for understanding the relationships between reason and emotion.[20] Brain imaging technology in particular has begun to provide insights into how players make choices in games. Scientists can now measure, in real time, which parts of the brain are activated in a particular task. An intriguing finding is that when a person is treated unfairly in a game, the part of the brain that "lights up" is the same region that is known to register disgust with repugnant tastes or odors.[21] Another interesting result from brain imaging is that even if inflicting vengeful punishment on a defector is costly, people derive real satisfaction from taking revenge.[22]

Although my work on the evolution of cooperation has been very well received and has inspired many novel applications by others, naturally, there have been criticisms as well. Many of these critiques and challenges have been useful in identifying the scope of my results, and suggesting new directions for research.

To my mind, the most important criticism is that a strategy of simple reciprocity such as TIT FOR TAT does poorly when there is the possibility that one player will misunderstand what the other player chose to do. To fix this, simple reciprocity needs to be leavened with a bit of generosity. To my knowledge, the first to point this out was Per Molander in 1985.[23]

The problem is serious: because when one player thinks the other just defected, the victim is likely to retaliate, and this can lead to a series of defections that can echo back and forth for a long time. In my design of the computer tournaments, there was no possibility of such misunderstandings. Yet some degree of misunderstanding is typical of most strategic interactions, and this can cause real trouble for TIT FOR TAT.

Although I wish I had fully appreciated this basic drawback to simple reciprocity earlier, I did not entirely ignore the problem. I did have an intuitive understanding of the problem that an occasional misunderstanding can cause. In fact, when I developed the policy implications in the *Evolution of Cooperation* I explicitly stated that "in many circumstances the stability of cooperation would be enhanced if the response were slightly less than the provocation."[24] The simplest way to include the possibility of misunderstanding in the iterated Prisoner's Dilemma is to allow some percentage—say 10 percent—of defections by the other player to go unpunished. Working with my postdoctoral fellow, Jianzhong Wu, we showed that if the original tournament had included some misunderstanding, a generous variant of TIT FOR TAT would have won the tournament anyway.[25] In the presence of some occasional misunderstanding, reciprocity still works well, provided it is accompanied by some generoslty—which means you have some chance of cooperating when you would otherwise defect.

In 1988, I had an opportunity to see how two sophisticated players would behave when they were told that the choice they made in the iterated Prisoner's Dilemma might occasionally not be implemented as intended. At a U.S.–Soviet conference on interdependence, I invited two of the participants to play in front of the audience of social scientists. The meeting took place during the time of Soviet president Mikhail Gorbachev's friendly overtures to the West. The Soviet player was Sergei Blagovolin, a specialist in nuclear strategy. The American was Catherine Kelleher, a professor and former member of the White House staff who specialized in international security affairs. I told them that each of their choices would have a one-in-six chance of being misimplemented, as when a civilian airliner went off course and entered Soviet airspace.

Both players would know after the fact whether their *own* choice had been misimplemented, but they would never know whether the *other* player's action was the intended choice or not. The American started off with a deliberate defection and cooperated only three times in nine moves. The Soviet player cooperated more, five times. In the debriefing afterwards, he attributed most of the American defections to misimplementation. When asked why, the Soviet player said that he expected Americans would be fairly cooperative, and that women, in particular, would be cooperative. The American, on the other hand, explained that she *expected* him to think this way. Therefore, she deliberately defected, correctly expecting that she would be forgiven in line with the very generous Soviet foreign policy at the time. The story illustrates a significant moral: noise calls for forgiveness, but too much forgiveness invites exploitation.

The need to dampen mutual recrimination is especially acute when trouble can start with a simple misunderstanding rather than a deliberate provocation. International politics is a prime example of a setting in which misunderstandings are both common and serious. We now have both theoretical results and laboratory experiments that demonstrate that a generous variant of TIT FOR TAT can cope with an occasional misunderstanding.[26]

A second criticism of my work has been that there are many possible outcomes of a repeated game like the iterated Prisoner's Dilemma. While mutual cooperation based upon simple strategies of reciprocity (such as TIT FOR TAT) is certainly one possible possibility, there are many others. The basic idea is that if the shadow of the future is strong enough, any possible outcome can be sustained as long as both players get at least the amount they can guarantee for themselves by defecting. This theoretical result is called the folk theorem because no one can remember who first thought of it. The Folk Theorem leaves open the questions of what kind of strategy one should use in a given context and what outcome is most likely to occur among sophisticated players. In my view, the many tests for robustness provided in the *Evolution of Cooperation* help to answer both of those questions.

A third criticism appeared in a *Nature* article entitled "A Strategy of Win-Stay, Lose-Shift That Outperforms Tit-for-Tat in the Prisoner's Dilemma Game."[27] With a title like that, I really wanted to understand the basis for the claim. The article reported a simulation study that included misperception. It found that under the particular circumstances of the simulation,[28] the most successful strategy is one that repeats its previous choice only when it gets one of the two highest payoffs, namely the temptation incentive for exploiting the other player or the reward for mutual cooperation. Unlike TIT FOR TAT, it defects after the other player suffers an exploitation and it cooperates after a mutual defection. The strategy of Win-Stay Lose-Shift dates back at least to the classic 1965 book on the Prisoner's Dilemma by Anatol Rapoport and Albert Chammah where it was called Simpleton because of its shortcomings.[29] For example, the strategy can easily be exploited by a player who always defects since dissatisfaction with a mutual defection will lead it to cooperate on the next move and its dissatisfaction with the resulting mutual defection will lead to another try at cooperation. The result is that Win-Stay Lose-Shift, when playing with a rule that always defects, will wind up alternating between the worst two payoffs: punishment for mutual defection and the sucker's payoff.

I was curious to see how Win-Stay Lose-Shift would do in the variegated environment of the second round of the computer tournament. I was particularly interested in how it would do in a noisy version of that environment in which one player could misunderstand the choice the other player had just made. Although the original rules were designed without regard to noise, these rules can still be useful as a setting for evaluating how new strategies will fare in a heterogenous noisy environment. Wu Jianzhong and I reran the sixty-three rules of the second round while adding four new strategies: a generous variant of TIT FOR TAT that cooperates 10 percent of the time after the other player has defected (GTFT), a contrite variant of TIT FOR TAT (CTFT) that avoids responding to the other player's defection after its own unintended defection (CTFT), Win-Stay Lose-Shift (WSLS), and a generous variant of Win-Stay Lose-Shift (GWSLS).[30] The result was that GTFT and CTFT did well in coping with noise (misunderstanding), but neither variant of Win-Stay Lose-Shift did well. Moreover, when we performed an ecological analysis of many simulated generations, we found that WSLS died out and CTFT came to dominate the population. Both results suggest that the WSLS is not a robust strategy presumably because it can teach others to defect all the time.

A final point about the claim that WSLS outperforms TIT FOR TAT is that the claim is based on a simulation using the unrealistic assumption that a payoff received in the distant future is as valuable as a payoff received immediately.[31]

In sum, criticisms of my work on cooperation left the basic arguments intact. My demonstration that cooperation can emerge in a world of egoists without central authority provides an optimistic counterpoint to Hobbes's famous assertion that without central authority, egoists would be condemned to a world where life was "solitary, poor, nasty, brutish and short.[32] A valid criticism of TIT FOR TAT is that it doesn't handle an occasional misunderstanding or misimplementation very well. This criticism was helpful in that it spurred me to work with Wu Jianzhong to reanalyze a "noisy" version of the second round of the tournament in which we found that the problem could be overcome by adding a little generosity or contrition. And the only strategy that claimed to be more effective than TIT FOR TAT proved to be easily exploitable by a highly uncooperative player.

Turning from the explicit criticisms of my research on the evolution of cooperation, others have noted that the iterated Prisoner's Dilemma is not the only important setting in which the evolution of cooperation can take place. This is a valid point, and their extensions of the paradigm have led to new insights. Martin Nowak and Karl Sigmund, for example, designed a game that allowed a player to share with its current partner the experiences it had with other players.[33] Having one's own behavior reported to others provided an incentive to develop a good reputation, thereby supporting cooperation. Another extension of the paradigm is to allow ostracism of an uncooperative player. David Hirshleifer and Eric Rasmusen showed how such ostracism can sustain cooperation when it might otherwise not be possible.[34] Robert Putnam studied whole networks of trust and reciprocity called social capital. His empirical research showed that such networks have been instrumental in sustaining cooperation in large groups.[35] In a combination of empirical and theoretical research, Elinor Ostrom showed how people engaged in exploiting a common resource pool such as a fishing ground can and do develop decentralized mechanisms to control their overuse.[36]

I too have explored various ways cooperation can evolve using extensions to the basic paradigm. With Ross Hammond, I modeled how visible markers of similarity can sustain in-group cooperation based on ethnocentrism.[37] Rick Riolo, Michael Cohen, and I have explored how such markers can sustain cooperation even in a single-move Prisoner's Dilemmas.[38] We also explored how structured networks of interaction can work.[39]

I was curious about what could be said about Prisoner's Dilemmas with more than two players, such as the problem of the famous "tragedy of the commons," in which allowing everyone to graze their sheep on the village commons led to overgrazing.[40] I knew that sometimes a norm can be powerful enough to sustain cooperation in large groups, but I wondered how and when such a norm could emerge and be sustained. One of my motivating examples was Alexander Hamilton's willingness to risk his life—and ultimately lose it—in accepting a duel because the norm supporting dueling was so powerful that he felt that refusing the confrontation would end his usefulness in public affairs.

To study norms, I adapted my usual technique of an agent-based model with strategies evolving over time. In this case, the strategies involved two factors: how bold an actor would be in taking advantage of others, and how vengeful an actor would be in punishing those who did take advantage. To keep the process from unraveling, I assumed that the probability of vengeance against exploiters was the same as against those who do not punish exploiters.

The result was the emergence not only of a norm against exploiting others but also a "metanorm" against those who did not support the norm itself.[41] The concept of secondary sanctions is an example of a metanorm. A good example of the metanorm of secondary sanctions is China's cautious support for Russia's 2022 invasion of Ukraine lest the powerful economic sanctions that have been imposed on Russia are imposed on China as well.

In my 1986 article on norms and metanorms, I included two cautionary observations that are even more relevant now: civil rights and civil liberties are as much protected by informal norms of what is acceptable as they are by the powers of the formal legal system, and tolerance of the opposition is a fragile norm that can have a great impact on whether a democracy can survive.

As we have seen, the basic paradigm of the evolution of cooperation has not only been widely applied, from viruses to nations, but it has also lent itself to a wide range of extensions from the ostracism of an individual to norms in whole societies. I have been gratified by the impact and endurance of my work, especially my work on cooperation.

Over the years, about a dozen people have told me they had changed the entire path of their career after reading *The Evolution of Cooperation*. Some of these people were studying or doing social science and were inspired to enhance their tool chest by developing their mathematical or computer skills. Others had a background in science or engineering and were inspired by the possibility that their talents could be used to contribute to a meaningful problem in the social sciences.

My work on cooperation as well as other themes that I'll discuss in the following chapters has received recognition in many ways. Among the formal awards are two that are especially meaningful to me. The first came in 2014 when I was awarded the National Medal of Science, which is designated as "the nation's highest honor for scientific accomplishment

Figure 3. Receiving the National Medal of Science from President Barack Obama, November 20, 2014

and leadership." While economists and psychologists had occasionally won the award, no political scientist had ever joined the ranks of the physical and biological scientists who have been the most frequent winners. For me, the most exciting part was going to the White House to be congratulated by President Barack Obama. As he placed the ribbon and medal around my neck, he whispered into my ear, "I'm proud of you." It was one of the high points of my life. It brought back the happy memory of my being congratulated for being a "promising young scientist" fifty years earlier by another hero of mine, President Kennedy.

Many stories of scientific success describe the process as fierce competition, but my own experience has been quite different. While I am certainly competitive, I am not cutthroat. Indeed, it is striking that the success in my tournaments reflects my own style of work: soliciting cooperation from others rather than trying to outdo them.

The year after receiving the National Medal of Science, I had another echo from my high school years: this time it was a repair of a rejection rather than the fulfillment of a prediction. I had set my heart on being admitted to study at Harvard, and now, fifty years later, I was given an honorary degree by the same institution. Only when I started receiving the alumni magazine soon thereafter did it sink in that I was now accepted. The ceremony itself took place at the commencement in front of 32,000 graduates and their proud friends and families. By a happy coincidence, my daughter Lily was being awarded her law degree at the same event, so I got a special cheer from her classmates when my name was announced.

PART IV

SELF-ORGANIZATION

Although I am best known for my work on the emergence of *cooperation* without central authority, it wasn't until I started writing this autobiography that I realized that many of my projects over my fifty-year career have been variations on the theme of the emergence of *organization* without central authority.

In chapter 12, I present my validated theories of how self-organization can happen in the context of diverse political parties in a parliamentary democracy when diverse political parties need to form a coalition large enough to command a majority of seats. In the international context, I examine how mutually antagonistic nations on the verge of war organize themselves into two competing sides. I also show how my theory of international alignments works in a completely different context to predict alignments of computer companies that compete over whose standards will prevail. I've been guided by a principle of mine that—despite mutual rivalries—politics actually tends to minimize the strangeness of bedfellows.

Chapter 13 offers models on social polarization, specifically dealing with how extreme polarization can be prevented, how ethnocentrism can so readily arise, and how distinct cultures can form in a process of local convergence resulting in global differences.

Chapter 14 uses analogous ideas to study the emergence of organization among the partially conflicting beliefs of a single person or group and shows how organized beliefs can be exploited by someone else for surprise and even deception.

CHAPTER 12

MINIMIZING THE STRANGENESS
OF BEDFELLOWS

Parliamentary Coalitions

My dissertation on conflicts of interest included a theory of how politics minimizes the strangeness of bedfellows.[1] To make the theory concrete, I chose to analyze coalition formation in a multiparty parliamentary democracy. My approach was to think about which parties would wind up forming a ruling coalition, rather than worry about the details of how political leaders might have gotten to that outcome. My prediction was that the coalitions that form will be the ones that minimize stress, where stress was operationalized as ideological distance between the parties. I used Italy from the time its democratic politics stabilized in 1953 after World War II to the time I carried out the research in 1969. I chose Italy for two reasons. First, the fact that it had eight political parties made it somewhat challenging to make predictions about membership in governing coalitions. Second, there were a lot of data to account for: namely, seventeen coalitions in this sixteen-year period.

Since I only knew the left-right ordering of the parties and not their exact position, I couldn't apply my quantitative measure directly. I could, however, predict that the coalition that actually formed would be big enough to govern but would have no unnecessary conflict of interest among its members. This implied that the coalition would have no greater breadth than necessary. I also predicted that the winning coalition would include any party that was between two members in the ideological positions of those two parties, since that would strengthen the coalition without adding any additional stress in the ideological range of the member parties. I called my theory minimal winning connected coalitions. I found that my predictions were more accurate than those of any of the other four published theories—all of which were based on zero-sum thinking that ignored the ideological differences among the parties.

I also noticed something interesting about the durability of the Italian coalitions. In the few cases where a coalition formed that had more conflict of interest than was necessary, it didn't last as long as those that did have minimal conflict of interest. In other words, when the pattern did not conform to my prediction, things fell apart relatively quickly. So even the failures of my theory turned out to provide additional support for the idea that conflict of interest helps explain how systems self-organize.

International Alignments

I have always been more interested in questions of war and peace than in the formation of parliamentary coalitions. So, in 1991, I expanded my theory of minimizing stress to see if I could predict the alignments of nations in the context of an impending war. I chose the example of the years before World War II, specifically 1936 to 1939, when seventeen European nations were in the process of aligning with or against each of the others. Looking prospectively, the eventual alliances were far from obvious since each of the three major powers—Britain, Germany, and the Soviet Union—had deep animosity toward the other two. As Churchill famously said when Britain and the Soviet Union finally aligned against Germany: "If Hitler invaded Hell, I would make at least a favourable reference to the Devil in the House of Commons."

Unlike in the case of Italian political parties, there was no single dimension that could account for the amount of stress that would result in any two given countries aligning on the same side. So I used what I took to be the five main sources of affinity or difference between countries: ethnic composition, religion, border disagreements, type of government, and any recent history of wars between them. The theory also

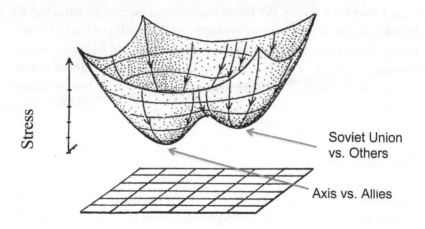

Stress

Soviet Union
vs. Others

Axis vs. Allies

Figure 4. Possible alignments on the eve of World War II

included national capabilities, assuming that a country would care more
about its alignment for or against a strong country compared to a weak
country.

There are over 65,000 possible two-sided alignments that seventeen countries can have. My mathematics education came in handy as I
recalled the beautiful ways in which I could conceptualize all these alignments as corners of a sixteen-dimensional hypercube, as represented in
the simplified figure above. The hypercube had one dimension for each
country indicating which of the two possible alignments that country
was in.[2] At the bottom is a two-dimensional representation of the various possible alignments, and on the vertical axis is the degree of stress
for each alignment.

The theory predicted that the alignments that formed would be the
ones that minimized stress. In other words, I was again predicting that
politics would *minimize* the strangeness of bedfellows. The predictions
were based on the tendency of an alignment to change if a country's
changing sides would lower stress, as shown in the vertical arrows of figure 4. Change in the alignment of countries continues until a local min-
imum was reached, namely, when no country could reduce its stress by
changing sides.

Working with Scott Bennett, then a graduate student in political science, I tested the theory. We based our predictions on 1936 data, and all but two of seventeen countries (Poland and Portugal) conformed to our theory. Since there were only 154 alignments that had the same or less stress, the odds of a prediction's being this good was only about one in two hundred.[3] All in all, a gratifying success for the stress minimization approach.

Business Alliances

Two years later, Scott and I were invited to present our research on international alignments at Michigan's business school. After my talk, two economists from the school, Will Mitchell and Robert E. Thomas, approached Scott and me. They told us that our work reminded them of the business coalitions that often form to compete over whose preferred standard will dominate an industry. They had in mind the specific case in which eight computer companies each joined one of the two coalitions that competed over which version of the UNIX operating system would prevail. We decided it would be fun to see if a theory of relations between countries could also account for relations between businesses.. We used exactly the same theory and simply plugged in the numbers for pairwise propensities to work together or compete. For example, we assumed that a company would find it more stressful to align with a company that was largely in the same market as it was, compared to a company that was mainly in a completely different market. We also took into account the relative importance of UNIX to each company. We found that the stress minimization application so useful for predicting military alignments was also successful at predicting a business alignment.[4]

CHAPTER 13

SOCIAL POLARIZATION

The previous chapter dealt with my research on who will work with whom. This chapter deals with how the actors themselves may change through their interactions with one another. The domains I chose to study were culture, ethnocentrism, and political attitudes.

Cultural Dissemination

Social scientists have long been puzzled by the observation that although people tend to become more alike in their beliefs, attitudes, and behavior when they interact, such differences never disappear. Social scientists have proposed many mechanisms based on disruptive external influences. But I had a hunch that stable global polarization could result even if there were nothing but a local influence toward convergence. Doing this would provide a new type of explanation of why we do not all become alike. Because the proposed mechanism can exist alongside other mechanisms, it can be regarded as complementary to older explanations rather than necessarily competing with them.

I started with two very simple principles about interaction: interaction is more likely between similar than between dissimilar individuals, and when interaction between two individuals does happen, it tends to reduce the differences between them. To study what would happen with two such simple rules, I needed a way to represent the things that might make two individuals similar or dissimilar. I had in mind differences

77

in language, religion, technology, style of dress, and so on. In general, I thought of culture as what is affected by social influence and I thought of the project as the study of the dissemination of culture.

To simulate this process with an agent-based model, I imagined a geography of 100 by 100 locations. Instead of individuals as the actors, I thought of the actors as homogeneous villages with one village in each location.[5] I started with five cultural traits (such as language), each of which had ten possible values (such as French and German), initially chosen at random. The dynamics couldn't be simpler: an actor interacted with a neighbor in proportion to the number of traits it shared, and if it did interact, it lessened its cultural difference with its neighbor by adopting the value of one of the traits on which it differed, if there were any differences.

My social influence model is very simple indeed. Its mechanism can be stated in a single sentence: with probability equal to their cultural similarity, a randomly chosen site will adopt one of the cultural traits of a randomly chosen neighbor. That's it.

The degree of polarization is measured by the number of different cultural regions that exist when no further change is possible. This happens when every pair of neighbors has either no differences between them or so many differences that they stop interacting.

One of exciting things about doing agent-based simulations is that you know what you put in, but you can be quite surprised by what comes out. In fact, there are three kinds of surprise. The first kind of surprise is quickly resolved, and you say to yourself, "I really shouldn't have been surprised. After all, the result is obvious now that I've seen it." The second kind of surprise is when the result is not at all obvious at first, but after some study you say to yourself, "Oh, now I get it. I now understand how this unexpected result was generated by the simulation of the agent-based model." The third level of surprise is when the result seems so counterintuitive that you say to yourself, "I don't believe it. There must be a bug in the program." In the case of the culture model, the counterintuitive result wasn't a bug at all—just an interesting discovery.

I learned that when considering the dynamics of a cultural system, one should distinguish between the number of different features and the number of traits that each feature can take. The takeaway is that even when the only source of social influence is that interactions reduce differences between neighbors, the effect can be local convergence but global polarization. An example would be the way regions of France with different dialects converged to share a common language, while adjacent regions in what is now France and Germany came to have mutually incomprehensible languages. While the process of local convergence within France had substantial top-down support, the bottom-up convergence process was also powerful.

Ethnocentrism

Ethnocentrism is a major cause of stress between groups. In the form of in-group favoritism, it is nearly universal. I wanted to see whether a simple agent-based evolutionary model could reproduce this well-known phenomenon and provide new insights into the development of ethnocentrism. Ross Hammond, then a graduate student at Michigan, had the same question.[6]

What would the model have to include? There would have to be at least one heritable trait on which group distinctions could be made, and the trait would have to have at least two observable variants: say, Orange and Purple. Evolutionary success would have to be based on some kind of interaction between the agents, so we resorted to my old friend, the Prisoner's Dilemma. To incorporate essential aspects of territoriality we made the propagation of strategies local in a two-dimensional space. To keep things as simple as possible, we dropped the usual premise of iteration and used a one-shot Prisoner's Dilemma. Then, the range of strategies could be just four possibilities: cooperate with everyone, be ethnocentric (i.e., cooperate only with those of one's own color), cooperate with no one, and cooperate only with those of the opposite color. Agents with low scores die, and agents with high scores reproduce to make a new agent with the same color and strategy, subject to mutation. Global stress is the amount of defection exhibited.

The result was that the Orange actors and the Purple actors became two coherent groups despite the fact that the colors, and the actors' strategies, were originally assigned at random. The two coherent groups each displayed a high level of both in-group favoritism and out-group defection despite the fact that cooperation with anyone (including those in one's in-group) was suboptimal in a series of one-move games. In fact, had it not been for the observable colors to help groups get established, evolution would have led to nearly all defections in the one-shot Prisoner's Dilemma. Instead, the overall rate of cooperation increased with the rise of ethnocentrism. The reason for high levels of cooperation in the emerging ethnocentric world was that defection mainly occurred only at the boundaries *between* in-groups.

Political Attitudes

My earlier work on polarization in 1997 and 2006 dealt with the dissemination of culture and the emergence of ethnocentrism, respectively. By 2016, political polarization in the United States and many other democracies was becoming an urgent matter. So when Stephanie Forrest told me about a project to recruit a dozen or so papers on this theme, I was definitely interested. The project was based on an idea from Simon Levin of Princeton to get the *Proceedings of the National Academy of Sciences* to publish a special feature. The novelty was that each article would entail a collaboration of at least one computer scientist and one social scientist. When Steph invited me to join her, I knew we'd have a good time since we'd already done so much together over more than thirty years: in 1987, when she was a computer science graduate student, she worked with me to simulate hypothetical future tournaments of the iterated Prisoner's Dilemma;[7] in 2006, she introduced me to an agent-based model of a growing tumor that got me started on cancer research; and in 2017, we published an article on cyber conflict.[8] Steph has always been a terrific collaborator. Among other things, she was ready and able to stop me from rushing ahead on a given model before we had established what was worth really knowing about the problem at hand.

Steph and I were concerned about two kinds of polarization (affective and ideological) that, if carried to extremes, can undermine democracy. Affective polarization is the extent to which members of one party dislike and distrust those of another. In the United States, affective polarization has been growing and is now a serious problem for democracy. Ideological polarization, on the other hand, reflects the extent to which political views are widely dispersed. Ideological polarization is already strong among elites but is less pronounced among the general public. We anticipated that ideological polarization among the US public would likely increase due to the already strong affective polarization, rising social inequality, and the growing partisanship of almost every issue. Therefore, we felt it was important to understand how to prevent the public from reaching dangerous degrees of ideological polarization.

To explore the process of polarization and how to prevent it, Steph and I invited her postdoctoral fellow, Joshua Deymude, to join us. We built an agent-based model starting with the well-established principle of homophily, namely that similar people are more likely to interact with each other than with dissimilar people.[9] The model also posited that interaction between similar actors reduces their difference while interaction between dissimilar actors increases their difference. Our analysis explored the polarizing effects arising from different levels of tolerance of other views; responsiveness to other views; exposure to dissimilar actors; multiple ideological dimensions, economic self-interest; and external shocks. The results suggested strategies for preventing, or at least slowing, the development of extreme polarization. While repulsion is often omitted from models of political polarization, we identified some circumstances in which repulsion between dissimilar actors can actually reinforce a moderate majority—thus reducing polarization as measured by the variance in the distribution of political attitudes.

CHAPTER 14

BELIEF SYSTEMS

Ever since graduate school, I've been interested not only in interactions *between* people but also what's going on *within* a person. For example, I used survey data to see how people's attitudes on policy issues related to each other. I found that even in the 1950s, people's views were organized along a pro- and antipopulism dimension that was even stronger than the liberalism–conservatism dimension.[10]

I tried developing a very abstract treatment of how beliefs might be organized. Although it was published in a major political science journal, it was just too abstract to get much uptake.[11]

A few years later, I came up with the idea of studying elites' belief systems as they ponder consequential choices. Since I was especially interested in foreign policy decision-making, I looked for records of high-level deliberations. I decided to focus on the causal arguments people made, and for this, I needed verbatim transcripts. No doubt my interest in reading transcripts of high-level discussions grew out of my childhood desire to eavesdrop on my parents and their friends after I was sent to bed.

I was able to locate transcripts from a cabinet-level committee, the 1918 British Eastern Committee. But I couldn't find archival material from a non-Western source for comparison. Eventually, I went to Japan and met with the archivist of the Foreign Ministry. When I explained that I was looking for verbatim transcripts and not just minutes of meetings, the archivist thought for a long time, and then looked at his shoes. I could tell that he couldn't think of anything suitable. Then he looked up hopefully and said, "Is that the only reason you've come to Japan?" Without thinking, I said, "Yes," but apologized when I realized that such a blunt response was very rude in a Japanese context. Next, I went to see Professor Taizo Takahashi, a professor at Hitotsubashi University whom I was told might be helpful. He asked for a few days to consider. Sure enough, in a few days, he asked me to come back. When I returned, he invited me in with a smile and asked two guests to join us. They were carrying a stack of documents that were exactly what I was looking for. I thanked them profusely, and after they left, I asked the professor what they had been quietly saying to each other as they entered. He replied, "Look: he's short just like us."

While I was waiting to hear back from Professor Takahashi I took in the sights of Tokyo. I couldn't speak Japanese, but I managed to identify a bus that was about to leave for the museum I wanted to visit. Along the route, it gradually filled up. Since I had gotten on at the start, I soon found myself crowded at the back. When we were just a few blocks from my destination, I very carefully weaved my way to the exit door at the front. As I did that, I got a lot of hostile looks from the other passengers. I knew that casual touches from strangers are generally unwelcome in Japanese culture, but I was doing my best. In fact, I timed it just right, getting to the front just as we reached my destination. Then, when I got off, so did everyone else. Only then did I realize that the museum was the end of the line. I realized what the other passengers must have been thinking: "The damned American just has to be the first off the bus." The incident brought home to me how easy it is for people of different cultures to misunderstand each other and unintentionally cause offense.

Back home, I analyzed the British and Japanese documents. To do this, I developed a method of extracting the causal arguments from the texts and graphing the network of cause-and-effect linkages used by each speaker.[12] To my surprise, the arguments were almost completely devoid of feedback loops (such as inflation leading to an increase in wages and higher wages in turn increasing inflation). Further research would have been necessary to determine whether the participants in these high-level meetings didn't recognize the existence of feedback loops, or were simply avoiding mentioning them in the interests of keeping their arguments straightforward. Unfortunately, this project was limited because it is difficult for human coders to reliably identify causal statements, and as far as I know automated text analysis programs have yet to solve the problem.

Another stab at understanding how a person's belief system is organized took the form of a study of historical analogies. Working with a talented postdoctoral fellow, Larissa Forster, we compiled a database of almost 900 historical analogies used in the nearly 500,000 words of coverage of three major events in newspapers of five different countries: 9/11; the 2008 terrorist attack in Mumbai, India; and the 2011 Egyptian revolution that started in Cairo's Tahrir Square.[13] We found the use of historical analogies to be ubiquitous in our sample, averaging about one per article. As expected, we found that when the author advocated for a policy choice, the chosen analogy was usually as similar as possible to the current situation. The similarity was useful in suggesting that actions in the current situation would be likely to lead to results analogous to the results of actions in the past. To our surprise, in the early stages of making sense of a surprising event, the chosen analogy was not necessarily very similar to the current situation. Instead, the chosen analogy was used to highlight a few of the features of the current event, to help shape the reader's understanding of the current event. My feeling about the project was that it was a lot of effort with not too much to show for it. But that's how research goes sometimes; you can't always predict what will work out.

Yet another approach to understanding how beliefs are organized is called "framing." The idea is that since alternative choices derive their meaning from their context, controlling the context in which a choice is offered provides a frame that can guide a decision in one direction or another. Daniel Kahneman won a Nobel Prize in economics for his work with Amos Tversky on framing. Scott Atran, Richard Davis, and I tried our hand at suggesting new frames to overcome some of the seemingly irreconcilable values involved in the Arab–Israeli conflict.[14] For example, in our interviews with leaders in the Middle East we found that even symbolic concessions such as an apology could mitigate the outrage that could be evoked by material offers that would be perceived as an insult rather than a compromise. It got us an article in *Science*, but I'm not sure if it got much traction in the Middle East.[15]

This brings me to yet another project on belief systems, one that actually did have some impact. It started with my fascination with deception—the manipulation of someone else's beliefs.

My favorite case of deception was how the British used double agents in World War II to help deceive Germany about where the cross-channel invasion would take place in 1944. By 1942, the British had discovered all the spies sent by the Germans, and they decided to build up the credibility of the captured German spies with valid reports up until the big event. The British acted cautiously until they were certain that their control of the German espionage system in Britain was complete. They decided to continue their caution in order to be able to exploit their resource to the fullest in one grand deception. The occasion was to be the Allied invasion of Europe. The British realized that they would incur a cost in the interim—a cost measured in terms of the damage done by the valid information that would have to be supplied to Germany through these agents in order to maintain their credibility. But the stakes involved in D-Day were so high that it was worthwhile to conserve these controlled agents until then. This patience was amply rewarded: the Germans fell for the grand deception and kept a large number of troops at Pas de Calais—even several days after the real attack at Normandy.[16]

I thought it would be interesting to develop a model to determine the best time to exploit a resource, such as a double agent, for deception. In thinking about the problem in abstract terms, I realized that the model could apply not only to a resource for deception but also to any resource for surprise including such things as secret weapons.

The mathematical model dealt with the question of when a resource for surprise should be employed by the attacker, knowing that its use today may well prevent it from being effective later.[17] The heart of the model was a trade-off between waiting until the stakes of the present situation are high enough to warrant the use of the resource and, on the other hand, not waiting so long that the vulnerability that the resource exploits might be discovered and repaired even if the resource had not yet been used. The question of when to use a resource is ultimately a matter of human judgment. My intention for the model was that it would help in making informed choices about the trade-offs involved in such a judgment.

A significant implication of the model was that when the stakes get very high, a great deal of surprise can be expected. Indeed, the victim may have mistakenly learned from previous, less important events that the absence of surprise suggests the other side doesn't have any resources for surprise, whereas the truth of the matter may be that such a resource has not yet been exploited because the stakes have not yet been high enough. This mistake may be one of the primary reasons why nations are so often overconfident about their ability to predict the actions of their potential opponents.

An unexpected implication was that the more an unsophisticated side can observe about the deceiving side, the more readily it can be deceived. The reason is simply that the more a side can observe, the more things can be presented as patterns of behavior in order to build up a false sense of confidence in the ability to predict. Thus, the presence of ever-more-sophisticated photographic and electronic reconnaissance devices may simply allow the observed side to obtain more and more resources for surprise. The resolution of this dilemma lies not so much in the further improvement of observational technology as in the more sophisticated understanding of the proper way to draw inferences from observations.

The model was actually used by Israel to make an important decision in 1982 about whether to use its secret technology at the onset of the Lebanon War. I heard this from retired General Itzik Ben-Israel, who was introduced to me by Scott Atran when we visited Israel in 2012. Ben-Israel explained that he had read my article and realized it could be applied to the current situation in which Israel needed to suppress the surface-to-air missiles deployed by Syria in the Bekaa Valley. At the time, he was chief operations officer for the Israeli air force. He told me that he used my model and estimated the values of the variables in the current situation. He derived the result that the secret weapons Israel had been keeping should be used rather than retained for a potentially bigger event later. His advice was contrary to Israeli doctrine that said that these new weapons should be retained for a general war on the scale of the wars in 1956 or 1967. The reason for not using the new weapons as soon as possible was that once the weapons were used, the enemy might well be able to take countermeasures, nullifying their advantage in future wars. However, he was able to convince his superiors that the current situation was sufficiently important to justify exploiting their ability to surprise the enemy. The operation involved innovative tactics and weapons.[18] The result was that Israel shot down eighty-seven Syrian fighter planes without losing a single one of its own.

According to a Czech general who was in Moscow at the time, the resources for surprise that the Israelis used in the Bekaa Valley air war showed the Soviets that Western technology was superior to theirs, and the conflict was part of the cascade of events leading to the collapse of the Soviet Union. Itzik Ben-Israel takes a more cautious view, saying, "I do believe that the continuous losses of Soviet armed Middle Eastern states against [American armed] Israel . . . was an important factor in accelerating the collapse of the Soviet Union."[19]

Another application of my model was suggested by my colleague William Zimmerman, an eminent Soviet expert. Together, we analyzed the Soviet press from 1945 to 1989 looking for lies about their own foreign policy behavior.[20] The results were consistent with the model in that the Soviets were careful to build up their credibility until the very important event of secretly installing nuclear missiles in Cuba in 1962. In the lead-up period, they denied doing any such thing, hoping to catch the US with a fait accompli.

The project had a valuable effect on my personal life. When Bill Zimmerman and I presented this work at our university's Russian Center, a graduate student from the History Department approached me afterward and said we were wrong because her research showed that the Soviets also lied about many things, such as not being anti-Semitic. I replied that we should have been clearer that we were only dealing with Soviet statements about foreign affairs. In any case, I like being challenged, and soon thereafter, I called her for a date. One thing led to another, and in 1982, Amy Saldinger and I were married.

Yet another application suggested itself decades later when cyber weapons were being developed, offering new opportunities for surprise in the form of so-called zero-day exploits that are the first to take advantage of previously unknown vulnerabilities. I began working with a postdoctoral scholar, Rumen Iliev, and we found it easy to adapt the model to cases such as the Stuxnet attack on Iran's nuclear program, the Iranian cyberattack on the energy firm Saudi Aramco, and the persistent cyber espionage carried out by the Chinese military.[21] Our publication received widespread attention including in *Science, Nature, ArsTechnica*, and the BBC World News Service. For example, a commentary on the *Science* website called it "a solid logical foundation for fresh thinking in the cybersecurity field."[22] The work was also reviewed in Chinese and Russian media.

Along the way, we identified an interesting case in which our model suggested that a resource for surprise was used sooner than would have been optimal. The case involved China's exploitation of its near monopoly on the production of rare-earth elements. Such elements are needed in the production of electronics, automobiles, and much else. The incident started on September 7, 2010, when a Chinese fishing trawler collided with a Japanese patrol ship near some disputed islands in the East China Sea. The Japanese took the trawler to Japan. On September 9 and again on September 12, the Chinese demanded that the captain and crew be released. The next day, Japan released the crew but continued to detain the captain. Tensions continued to escalate, and on September 21, China abruptly halted its exports of rare earth materials. Because China controlled 97 percent of the world's exports of rare earth elements, and Japan imported one half of that supply, the effects on Japan were immediate and drastic. Japan complained that this was economic warfare and released the captain within three days. China waited a month to restore exports to most of the world, and two months before restoring exports to Japan.

After this demonstration of economic coercion, Japan, the United States, and others invested in the production of rare-earth elements outside of China so as to never be subject to the same threat again. The Chinese dominance of the market for rare earth elements gave them a resource to cause substantial pressure on other countries, but like many resources for surprise it was perishable since it was relatively easy for the dependent countries to build up stockpiles of rare earths. Indeed, that's what these countries did after China's cutoff in 2010.

Although the release of the trawler captain was important to China, it is hard to see how the stakes in 2010 were greater than they would be in other situations that might arise in the not-too-distant future. Second-guessing a nation's choice is always problematic, but our model strongly suggests that the Chinese would have been better off had they had the

patience to wait for a situation with much higher stakes before their surprising deployment of their perishable resource for economic coercion.

Having described my wide-ranging work on cooperation and self-
organization, I'll now turn to my adventures in research on the reason for
sexual reproduction and the way in which cancer can usefully be viewed
as social dysfunction.

PART V

SEX AND CANCER

CHAPTER 15

THE REASON FOR SEXUAL REPRODUCTION

I have worked on political, economic, and social issues, and even cooperation in biological systems, but I never expected to work on the reason for sexual reproduction or the ways in which cancer grows out of control.

My research on sexual reproduction started this way. About five years after Bill Hamilton and I collaborated on the evolution of cooperation in biological systems, Bill told me about a truly amazing theory he was developing. By that time, Bill had taken a very prestigious position at Oxford, and we still kept in touch and shared news regarding our current interests. Bill's theory proposed an answer to one of biology's largest unresolved puzzles: Why have most large animals and plants evolved to reproduce sexually? Sexual reproduction has up to a twofold cost, since only half the population has offspring. What might be the advantage of sexual reproduction that is so great that it can overcome this twofold cost compared to asexual reproduction?

Among theories competing to explain this puzzle there was already a serious contender, and its leading advocate was the Russian geneticist Alexey Kondrashov. Kondrashov's explanation was based on the possibility that sexual reproduction might be helpful for bearing the cumulative burden of many generations of deleterious mutations. But Bill's theory was completely different. Put simply, he thought of sexual reproduction as an adaptation to resist parasites. This struck me as a totally bizarre but nevertheless intriguing idea.

Bill's reasoning was that parasites are ubiquitous, and their short life spans give them the advantage of being able to adapt quickly to an ever-changing host population. If the host population reproduced *asexually*, a line of parasites that had evolved to mimic the genetic markers on the cells of one host would automatically be well adapted to mimic the genetic markers of its offspring. On the other hand, if the hosts reproduced sexually, their offspring would not be virtual copies of either of their parents and thus would not be as vulnerable to a line of parasites that had evolved to match the genetic loci of one parent or the other.

Bill explained to me that there was a serious problem with convincing others that his theory could, in fact, account for the up to two-for-one burden of sexual reproduction. The problem was that the equations that described the process were totally intractable when there were more than two or three genetic markers. Yet Bill's whole idea relies on there being so many genetic markers that it would not be a trivial task for the parasites to match them. When I heard this, I responded to Bill with something like, "No problem. I know a method to simulate the evolution of populations with a lot of genetic markers. The method is called the genetic algorithm, and I've already used it to simulate a population of individuals each of whom has seventy genes."

I explained to Bill that a computer scientist, John Holland, had been inspired by the success of biological evolution in finding "solutions" to difficult problems by means of competition among an evolving population of agents. Based on the evolutionary analogue, including the possibility for sexual reproduction, Holland developed the genetic algorithm as an artificial intelligence technique. I could simply turn this technique around and help Bill simulate biological evolution, with or without sex. Since Bill was used to thinking in terms of heterogeneous populations of autonomous individuals, he readily grasped the idea of agent-based modeling. He also grasped without difficulty that an agent-based simulation was capable of demonstrating that certain assumptions are sufficient to generate certain results, even if the same results could not be proven by mathematical deduction.

Together with a computer science graduate student, Reiko Tanese, Bill and I built an agent-based model with two coevolving populations: hosts with long life spans, and parasites with short life spans. Our model specified that when a parasite interacted with a host that had markers similar to its own, it could kill the host and reproduce. In the simulation, the parasite population would tend to evolve to concentrate in the region of the "genetic space" where there were many hosts. Thus, successful hosts tended to suffer from increasing numbers of deadly parasites, reducing the numbers of those previously successful hosts. Meanwhile, other types of hosts with very different genetic markers might thrive. Then the process would repeat itself as the population of parasites tracked the ever-changing population of hosts. The system would always be out of equilibrium.

Bill was pleased with the results of our agent-based simulations. In his memoirs,[1] he reported feeling that

> the notion I had started with, that even against sex's full halving inefficiency the problem could be solved by looking at the need of a population to manoeuvre against its many rapidly evolving parasites, with these differentiating resistance tendencies at many host loci (the more the better), had been vindicated.

> Once Reiko under Bob's guidance had done the program, I experimented with it by e-mailing her or Bob with requests for chosen runs. At one point I visited the University of Michigan at Ann Arbor and worked for a fortnight intensively on modifications to the program with Reiko—this came after a bad patch of misunderstandings and unpromising runs that had caused us all to become somewhat pessimistic.

Unfortunately, the collaborative development of an agent-based model can be vulnerable to misunderstanding. In our case, the problem arose while we were exploring different ways to model host–parasite interaction. At one point, Bill sent an email from Oxford asking Reiko and me to undo our recent changes and try something else, which he described. It wasn't until a month or so later that Bill noticed the unpromising runs might have happened because our simulation program did not quite do what he had in mind. We eventually traced the problem to a misunderstanding about whether Bill's request to remove our recent changes referred to the previous day's work, or the previous week's.

In Bill's words,

Daily Reiko sprinkled me and Bob, like tender house plants, with her floppy disks bearing her updated codes....

[Once the debugging was completed] our model achieved results that others had stated impossible with the tools we were allowing ourselves. Many of the dragons that had oppressed individual-advantage models in the past seemed to us to be slain.... Our explicit modeling of a large number of loci in a Red Queen situation[2] certainly was [new] and the increase of stability of sex that came with the growth of numbers of loci made the most dramatic feature in our results.

It is the paper that I regard as containing the second most important of all my contributions to evolution theory. That second joint paper of 1990 (actually mainly written some three or so years before) was to be the first model where sex proved itself able to beat any asexual competitor immediately and under very widely plausible assumptions.

As I noted earlier, my earlier collaboration with Bill Hamilton on cooperation in biological systems was accepted for publication with little problem. Just the opposite was true of our second collaboration. We had a hard time publishing our simulation of Bill's theory that sexual reproduction could be an adaptation to resist parasites.

First, we tried *Nature*, a leading scientific journal closely followed by biologists of all sorts. The referees had many complaints, chiefly about the robustness of our results. Therefore, we did many more runs under a broad range of parameters to show that the explanation worked under a wide range of realistic conditions. We thought our second try had fully answered the referees' concerns.

Nevertheless when the revised paper went back to the referees with these new experiments included, but with no change to our centralizing of the Homo-like life history, we found all our new points left uncommented and the manuscript rejected by the referees even more curtly than before. Two of them indeed dug out new objections they hadn't thought of first time and claimed to see no substantial changes in the rest.

After our revised version was rejected by *Nature*, we submitted our paper to *Science*, another leading scientific journal widely read by biologists. We were also rejected by *Science,* which left us a little discouraged. As Bill describes it:

> Failing with these I sent it in a preliminary way to an editor of the Royal Society journals to see if they would be interested, but the comments I received were as discouraging as the rest. It particularly shamed me to have to tell Bob that even the society that supported me in general believed me to be over the hill on this topic....

> One of the puzzles about the dislike, even contempt, the work... seemed to arouse in my evolutionary peers is that it was as if we had been unable to explain what we were thinking.... And yet while one referee praised our style, another described the paper as written very badly; because neither said anything good about the ideas or content I presume that even the one that liked the writing found it a kind of eloquent twittering.

> The only intelligible claim in [one review] was that we had not reported on any simulations outside the range we had studied in detail.... If one criticized every paper studying some feature of one-locus population genetics, for example, on grounds that it hadn't yet probed into even just possible two-locus complications (or hadn't reported having done so), a substantial fraction of the literature of population genetics would have stayed unpublished.

> Our statement that we had tested the model much more widely than we covered in the states we reported evidently wasn't believed, as also was the case with our description of the model. Several referees said this wasn't adequate; and yet it was quite as thoroughly described as models usually are in papers whose results rely on simulation.... [In fact] a subsequent team (Richard Ladle and Rufus Johnstone, later joined by Olivia Judson) reproduced and extended our model purely [from] the paper's specification. Ladle and Johnstone did not even tell me they were working on this until our major results had been verified.

> Bill was surprised by the difficulties we were having.

The above record of rejections probably actually isn't long compared with some that much more revolutionary yet valid papers have received from journals. What, for example, about the attempts of Alfred Wegener to publish on continental drift, or Ignaz Semmelweiss to publish on puerperal fever, or Richard Altmann on the symbiotic origin of the mitochondrion? On the other hand, at the time we were submitting neither Bob nor I was an unknown scientist and neither of us had a reputation for mistaken or trivial ideas. The number of suspicious and hostile referees we found had come, therefore, as a considerable surprise.

... my efforts to remould [our simulation] to appease the latest whims of referees ... never worked: the referees always had new objections; dislike for our solution seemed to be unbounded.

Nevertheless, we were dogged in our efforts. We kept revising the paper to take into account, as best we could, the reviewers' criticisms. Why was our agent-based model such a hard sell? It was not because our model was less realistic than analytic models of evolution that had already been published, or that our work didn't break new ground, or that the problem was not important. So what was it? Bill thought about it this way:

Simulation in itself admittedly isn't understanding and various previous papers, including some of my own ..., had already drawn attention to the kinds of possibilities we were now testing. The simpler analytical discussions and models, however, including again my own, all had had severe snags and none showed any chance to be general. Besides treating many loci and many parasites at once—obviously much closer to the real situation (and the importance of our studying truly many loci, not just three or four, cannot be overstated)—we had brought in a variable life history that I consider to be much more realistic than is typical in most evolutionary modelling. ...

Nor could anyone pretend that this theme of evolution of sex was a narrow one nor of specialist interest only: from Erasmus Darwin to the present time, sex has repeatedly been saluted as one of biology's supreme problems, perhaps its very greatest. Hence Bob Axelrod and I at first believed that our model, with its realism and its dramatic success under conditions others had deemed impossible for it, was virtually sure to be acceptable to one of the major general scientific journals such as *Science* or *Nature*.

We suspected that part of the problem was that the reviewers were threatened by our application of Bill's theory to the case of human-like organisms—organisms similar to the reviewers themselves. It may not have been easy for them to accept that their own sexuality derived from the selective pressure of parasites.

Since we wanted to demonstrate that his theory could explain sexual reproduction in humans, Bill thought it was vital to include the salient characteristics of human reproduction. In particular, he wanted to include the fact that humans are not fertile for the first dozen or so years of their life. I, however, wanted our model to be as simple as possible to make it easier to understand and appreciate. This was the only significant disagreement we ever had. Since it was Bill's theory and Bill's audience, I deferred to his preferences. So one reason our model might have been so hard to sell is that it included some realistic details that may have obscured the basic logic of the simulation. On the other hand, Bill was probably right that had we *not* included these details, the reviewers would complain that we had not demonstrated that the theory could account for sexual reproduction in humans. Sometimes you just can't win.

After our rejections at *Science* and *Nature*, we were pleased that we had no trouble publishing in the *Proceedings of the National Academy of Sciences of the United States of America*.[3] This was our work's fifth version! At last, two reviewers saw the point of our paper, and one was even enthusiastic. The paper received wide attention, and Hamilton's theory is now regarded as one of the leading explanations for why sexual reproduction is so common despite its up to twofold cost.

In the end, Bill Hamilton gave his life to science. In 2000, despite the risks, he went to the depths of the Congo jungles to gather the evidence he needed to test a theory about the origin of AIDS. He contracted a virulent form of malaria that proved fatal. Who knows what additional great contributions to biology he could have made had he lived longer.

CHAPTER 16

CANCER AS SOCIAL DYSFUNCTION

For over twenty years, I had seen the potential for cooperation almost everywhere I looked, but I never expected to find it in cancer. Here's the story.

In 2006, I visited Stephanie Forrest, who years earlier had worked with me as a research assistant to apply the genetic algorithm to study the evolution of strategies in the iterated Prisoner's Dilemma.[4] We had kept up with each other, spending time together at the Santa Fe Institute and at the University of New Mexico where she was a distinguished computer scientist. We talked about common interests, such as protecting people's privacy.

As an aside, Steph asked if I would be interested in seeing an agent-based simulation of tumor growth that she was working on.[5] A student of hers had developed a three-dimensional visual display so that you could see how a tumor mass developed over time as cells divided and mutated. It was fascinating to watch the simulated blood vessels being recruited by the tumor cells to grow in their direction. As the blood vessels grew closer, the tumor cells were able to get more than their fair share of the oxygen and nutrients that all cells need to grow and divide. Each different kind of mutant cell was represented with a different color. You could rotate the image in three dimensions. Especially neat: when you clicked on a cell, all the cells *not* of that type would become transparent so that you could see inside the simulated tumor.

Having worked on many agent-based models, I saw what a wonderful toy Steph had.[6] I asked what assumptions were built into the simulation, and she told me it was based on a widely cited paper called "Hallmarks of Cancer."[7]

When I went home, I took a look at the paper. I was clearly in *way* over my head. But I did get the general idea, which is that cancer results from an accumulation of mutations in a single cell line. These mutant cells achieve new capabilities, until one cell type is eventually able to reproduce without being subject to all the controls usually provided by the host. The literature typically did not explicitly say that a single cell line must have all the hallmarks of cancer, but this seemed to be the implicit assumption.

Although I couldn't articulate it at the time, I had some vague idea that if different lines of tumor cells could overcome different defenses, they might be able to cooperate to overcome all those defenses together even though none would overcome *all* of the defenses on its own. Years later, I came up with this analogy: it's like saying a pair of robbers can specialize. Suppose one knows how to disable the alarm, and the other knows how to break the lock. If the two robbers work together, neither has to overcome all the defenses alone. Their ability to get away with a crime can be seen as a failure of the social order. Likewise the ability of a tumor to escape all the body's protections is a kind of social dysfunction. With cancer, my idea was that no single tumor cell line had to be able to overcome all the body's defenses. Perhaps this could account for the difficulty of controlling tumors—and perhaps this might even suggest a new approach to cancer therapy.

My brother Dave happens to be a geneticist and cancer researcher. We have a long-standing joke about whether I could cure war before he cured cancer. Putting this sibling rivalry aside, the next time I saw Dave, I tried out my nebulous idea. Dave didn't laugh at me. And I'm grateful for that. Instead of dismissing my idea, he took the time to search the literature and found that nobody had looked at cancer quite that way before.

With that encouragement, and with Dave's help, I decided to learn some of the basics of cancer, and to start to learn the specialized language that cancer researchers use. I found that most cancer research is focused on the precise role of hundreds, if not thousands, of specific kinds of molecules. But as the details accumulate, some researchers were starting to express a real need for an additional organizing principle that could help make sense of the details. Perhaps Dave and I could make some progress at that level. And perhaps I could export a little social science thinking to medicine. I thought this was a challenge that would be fun to pursue.

Since Dave was pretty busy, I approached an oncologist at my own university, Kenneth Pienta. Ken was a coauthor with Steph Forrest on the agent-based model of cancer article with which I was so impressed. Steph said that he was receptive to new theoretical approaches to cancer. Like Dave, he didn't laugh when I told him my idea about cooperation among tumor cells.

It didn't take Ken long to understand that game theory could be applied at the cellular level. The new idea is that when a cell produces, for its own needs, products that can diffuse over some distance, it automatically helps nearby cells as well. So if two different cell types can each overcome different defenses in each other's neighborhood, they might both be able to propagate faster than cells that don't cooperate. For example, one cell type might use a diffusible product to overcome the control on how much blood is supplied to the neighborhood, and a different nearby cell type might be able to elicit more than the normal amounts of a specific protein that promotes a cell's growth. In that case, both cell types could propagate faster than either could alone.

We still had to work out the specifics of cooperation among tumor cells. Our task got a lot easier once we realized that when a tumor cell protects itself by making some diffusible product, it not only unavoidably helps the nearby cells, but it does so at no cost to itself. In other words, cooperation among tumor cells could result simply from each cell type doing what is best for itself. So we didn't have to worry about strategies or reciprocity or anything like that. In fact, the situation was about as conducive to cooperation as you can get: each cell just has to do what works for itself. In game theory terms, the interaction is not a Prisoner's Dilemma, requiring strategies, but simply by-product mutualism.

So far, so good. But could Ken, Dave, and I refine our ideas enough to make them meaningful and perhaps even useful to others? I decided to study cancer seriously so that I could help develop our ideas. It was an uphill struggle since cancer takes so many different forms, each with a wide variety of biochemical processes at play. While working with Ken and Dave, I sometimes felt that I was like someone speeding along in a car trying to maintain control with only a single finger on the steering wheel.

After a lot of hard work, we were able to show that the cooperation hypothesis is consistent with the known facts about cancer; it helps explain things that hadn't been understood before, and it suggests testable predictions. We also suggested that our approach might be relevant to cancer therapy because of the possibility of interrupting the cooperation between tumor cells.

We showed our paper to a few other cancer researchers and got very positive feedback. They said, in effect, "Hey, it's obvious *after* you say it." But when we submitted it for publication, we got a flat-out rejection. I've gotten my share of rejections, but every time it seems like a kick in the stomach, and I wonder why I'm in this academic business after all. This time, the reviews were highly contradictory: one said everyone *knew* this already, and the other said it was absolutely *impossible*.

After we picked ourselves up off the floor, we revised the paper to clarify exactly what was new, and why it wasn't impossible that our account was correct. That did the trick, and we were able to publish it in a major journal.[8]

As time has passed, it has been very gratifying to see that our speculation about cooperation among tumor cells has since been confirmed in the laboratory.[9] Moreover, in 2019, the National Cancer Institute posed nine "provocative questions" for possible funding, including the role of cooperation during cancer initiation and development.

While Ken Pienta is hardly a neutral observer, this was his assessment from 2013: "The theory of cooperation within the cancer ecosystem has gained tremendous traction in the last few years. Experiments have been performed that have proven that cooperation exists between cancer cells as well as between cancer cells and host cells to facilitate tumor growth. The work is causing a paradigm shift in thinking about tumorigenesis."[10]

Ken has since moved to Johns Hopkins University, and I have continued to collaborate with him and his colleagues, focusing on ideas that go beyond my hypotheses about cooperation among tumor cells. For example, Ken and I published an article presenting our view of cancer as a failure of cooperation that can be viewed as social dysfunction among the cells of the body.[11] It's been a privilege and a pleasure for me to work with

Ken and his colleagues. Ken himself is an extraordinary scientist who enriches the understanding of cancer by drawing on perspectives from fields as diverse as adaptive systems, game theory, and ecology as well as genetics and evolution. He designs lab experiments, conducts clinical trials, and leads overlapping teams of researchers from a dozen universities around the world.

I have continued to contribute to Ken's research on the importance of giant cells that are observed in the tissue of some chemotherapy treated patients. Ken had been studying them as possible sources of resistance of cancer cells to chemotherapy, the recurrence of cancer after therapy, and the metastatic spread of cancer cells to different organs. Ken's research group at Johns Hopkins has been collaborating with Robert Austin in the Physics Department at Princeton to generate and study these giant drug resistant cells in the laboratory.[12] Indeed, we found evidence that giant cells, which can be up to thirty times the size of other tumor cells, are key actuators of the spread of cancer throughout the body.[13] The current goal is to determine if these giant tumor cells have unique vulnerabilities that can be targeted to provide a new form of cancer therapy.

One may wonder what a political scientist like me has had to offer to a team of cancer researchers once they moved beyond my familiar bailiwick of cooperation. Well, I did have a long-term interest in evolutionary thinking, although I was new to cancer studies. I can still try to follow their lab experiments, and, as an outsider to the field, I persist in asking naïve questions about the completeness of the reasoning behind the conclusions they draw from their observations. I can also suggest new experiments to try from time to time, and I can help edit their manuscripts to turn what looks like a lab report into a story with a coherent narrative. In any case, they keep inviting me back, and I'm now the coauthor with Ken Pienta and his team on six cancer papers.[14]

PART VI

Outside the Ivory Tower

I've taken many opportunities to be active outside of the ivory tower, chiefly in the realm of international peace and security. Some of my engagement was direct activism including electoral campaigning and organization of protests against the war in Vietnam. Some of it was participation in a host of governmental and nongovernmental meetings in conflict zones. Some of it was centered around meetings with academics and scientists from other countries to deal with issues such as arms control and norms for cyber conflict. It's hard to say whether my activism and service beyond academia had discernible real-world impact, but it was highly engaging, and informed both my research questions and my teaching. These activities provided me with experiences that I could use to think about the fundamentals underlying how political leaders think about their world, and as well as what might promote cooperation or at least lessen the chance of unnecessary conflict. These experiences were also, by and large, a lot of fun for a curious person like me: they involved meeting very interesting people, often from other cultures and other occupations, and working together with them on things worth doing.

CHAPTER 17

OPPOSING THE VIETNAM WAR

After virtually completing my PhD dissertation in March 1968, I joined the full-time national staff of the McCarthy for President campaign as a volunteer. Senator Eugene McCarthy ran for president to oppose Lyndon Johnson's continuing escalation of the war in Vietnam. Since I, too, opposed the war, I thought this was a good opportunity to get out of the ivory tower for a while. When I joined the national staff, my main job was to do research for his speechwriters. I spent five happy months campaigning in primaries across the country.

As the Indiana primary drew closer, I was sent to Oregon to do advance work to prepare the national staff for the local scene there. While I did a lot of issue research, the most helpful thing I did was to collect the phone numbers of all local staff for use by the national staff. A few days after Senator McCarthy and the rest of the national staff came to Oregon, the speechwriters were so busy that they asked me to do a job they would normally do: draft a press release on environmental policy. I wrote a set of bullet points on specific issues, such as the water quality of the Willamette River. When the senator read it as I sat on a couch next to him, he said, "This looks like something Bobby would have written." He was referring to Bobby Kennedy, his opponent in the Oregon primary. His likening what I drafted to something Bobby Kennedy could have written wasn't a compliment coming from a person who was better known as a sardonic wit than a policy wonk. I realized how naïve I had been to write something like that. But we had no time to redo it, so he just shrugged his shoulders and approved the press release as written.

I got a lot out of working in the national staff of a presidential campaign. For one thing it was my first experience with a large, mostly volunteer operation, showing that it is possible to harness the energy of local groups for a common purpose. The contrast with my summer internship in the Pentagon three years earlier taught me that both bottom-up as well as top-down organizations can be effective in coordinating work. I also came to appreciate that my wide range of activities was often motivated not only by curiosity and the desire to make a contribution but also as a means to develop knowledge and skills that might be useful in future work both inside and outside the ivory tower.

During the course of the campaign, I made what may well have been my largest contribution to public affairs. And I did so by keeping my mouth shut at a critical moment.

Here's what happened. In April 1968, North Vietnam announced a list of cities where it would consider holding peace talks with the United States. Shortly thereafter, the United States announced a different list of cities it would consider. I thought that I should alert Senator McCarthy so that he could criticize the president for not accepting any of the sites that North Vietnam had proposed. But first I wanted to satisfy my curiosity about what might have gone into making those two lists. I soon realized that the lists included every country in which both sides had embassies—except for one country, France. That's when it occurred to me that the US was tacitly signaling to North Vietnam that Paris would be acceptable, and was doing so in a way that avoided putting Hanoi in the position of accepting or rejecting a US proposal. (Years later, a declassified document confirmed that my analysis was correct.)[1] I further realized that if Senator McCarthy criticized President Johnson for leaving France off the list, the president might feel the need to reject anything that Senator McCarthy proposed. So I kept my mouth shut, and pretty soon, the two sides agreed to meet in Paris.

After Richard Nixon was elected president, my other major activity against the war was to help organize the March on Washington scheduled for Saturday, November 15, 1969. The organization I joined, the Moratorium, was building on teach-ins and nonviolent antiwar demonstrations that had been taking place all across the country. We were now hoping for the largest demonstration ever to be held in Washington, DC to date. And it turned out to be just that, with the crowd conservatively estimated to be over 250,000.

I arrived in Washington a week before the scheduled march. The Moratorium was in the process of sending out notices to the 12,000 people on their mailing list. I joined in the collating, stuffing, addressing, stamping, and sealing. But I quickly shifted to concentrate on the contingencies that no one was worrying about as they remained focused on the complicated logistics of the march. I developed a list of potential disasters and then wrote up a checklist about things to do including coordinating with the police, developing procedures to thwart troublemakers, and negotiating with the city. I was soon the local expert on security.

With less than a week to go, chaos was close at hand. We had yet to nail down speakers who could draw large crowds, we had yet to secure a permit for the march, there was virtually no housing for the tens of thousands expected to descend on DC, no plan for shuttle transportation and parking, and virtually no money. And many of the organizers were still not taking security too seriously until the evening before the march, when five big men wearing Nazi armbands barged past the receptionist and came up to our offices—supposedly to help with our leafleting. They were spontaneously met by my favorite tactic: namely, a cluster of people so large and compact that no one could move. Of greater concern to me were the Yippies, headed by the notorious Abbie Hoffman, the radical who was noted for his provocative activities. At one point, he came to me to see if he could promote the potentially violent march that the Yippies were separately planning. He wanted our leaflets to endorse it. When I explained that that wasn't going to happen, I got the most hateful stare I've ever experienced.

Once we had the permit for the march, it was time to get serious about coordination with the police, so I went to see the city police. The deputy chief of police for special operations proved very helpful. He went so far as to give me a copy of the twenty-seven-page police plan for the march. The head of the tactical unit was a polite, cheerful guy whose attitude was that if things went nicely, that was fine, but if anything went wrong, his force would be quite sufficient to set it back in place. On the other hand, the inspector for the traffic division regarded demonstrations as only so much traffic to be efficiently moved. He even explained that keeping the buses away from the staging area would not only prevent injuries but would also "make for a nice photograph of a large, compact mass of people, which is what you want."

Perhaps the strangest aspect of the march was that just as the Moratorium was trying to make it come off without a hitch, so was Nixon's White House. The contribution of the White House was a "rumor center." This was a facility in the municipal building next door to the city command post. During periods when civil order is threatened, the mayor and key people from various city and federal agencies sit in a command post in the combination city hall and police headquarters where they can stay in touch with all developments. On this occasion, they were worried about violence, so they set up an additional facility to be jointly staffed by the Moratorium people and the government people. Within a few hours, those who represented the government and those who were out to discredit it were working interchangeably to have a peaceful march.

The facility had a radio transmitter with fourteen walkie-talkies on an assigned frequency. We had our own set of walkie-talkies on the citizens' band for the marshals' operation, but as expected, they were often jammed with static and deliberate interference.

The facility went into operation Thursday night when the March Against Death started. This was the preliminary march that started at Arlington Cemetery and proceeded single file to the White House, where each marcher read the name of one war dead and then to the Capitol where each marcher dropped a placard with a dead person's name into a coffin.

The first message we received was aerial, and we noticed it from our Arlington Cemetery staging area: two observation helicopters were flying in low circles. I told Dick Blumenthal (of the White House staff) that I wanted to talk to him about the helicopters. I told him about the helicopters that sprayed tear gas over Berkeley. I also explained the difference between small spotter helicopters that are used by police and the National Guard for observation and the medium-sized helicopters that can be used to spray gas. He listened and then walked next door. Within five minutes, one helicopter had gone away, and the other was flying circles much further away.

That evening, I was out watching the Yippie rally led by Abbie Hoff-

man that was in the process of circling the Justice Department's building. The Yippies were yelling that they were going to "levitate" it. Within
minutes, 150 officers of the Civil Disturbance Unit (tactical squad) filed
out of the Smithsonian Natural History Museum across the street from
me and took up positions along the side of the Justice Department. It
took only a few more minutes for the head of the procession to get back
around to where I now stood. The building was totally encircled by the
Yippies, contrary to the conditions of their permit. Once again, this was
a demonstration the Moratorium wasn't sponsoring and therefore we
decided to keep our marshals away from it; we didn't want an association
with the Yippies' march that we presumed would turn violent.

The main group was now stopped in front of Justice, on Constitu-
tion Avenue, leaving me with several hundred bystanders and five police
personnel with almost nothing to see. But it wasn't lonely for very long.
The deputy chief of police drove up and got out to walk around our aban-
doned street corner. I knew from the police plans he had given me two
days before that he was personally commanding the Civil Disturbance
Unit that day. So I reintroduced myself and told him that now I was
with the liaison group in the municipal building, and I asked if I could
stick with him, figuring that he would be where the action was, and an
observer could do no better than stand next to the man on the spot who
was giving orders to the police. He gave his permission, and I reported
the breakup of the Yippie march to our headquarters at the municipal
building and was congratulated on my luck at being there to witness it.

Just as it was getting obvious that things were getting tense around
the corner, the deputy chief called the Civil Disturbance Unit to come
over to where he was. He formed the twenty-five officers in a line across
the width of the street and started marching them toward the demonstration, the fringe of which could be seen just around the corner of the
Justice Department building a short block away.

There I was, alongside the deputy chief, twenty feet ahead of the
slowly marching Civil Disturbance Unit, with the crowd of demonstrators a few hundred feet away and an empty street between us.

"Don your gas masks," said the deputy to his men.

I called that in, and politely asked the deputy as we went along, "Have
you got a spare gas mask?"

Well, he didn't, so I walked back through the moving police line to a police car to ask them for one. But everyone carried only one for personal use. I asked a senior White House aide if he had an extra. But he was in the same boat, except that he hadn't even started looking yet. He looked at me as if to say, "Gee, you're a cautious fellow, aren't you?" It didn't require an answer, because the "pop, pop" of tear gas grenades started just about then.

Unfortunately, the wind was blowing our way, so I got my first real exposure to tear gas. I had managed to avoid the stuff the year before at the Democratic National Convention in Chicago when the police attacked demonstrators with what an official report later described as a "police riot." I managed to avoid tear gas through three major crises at Berkeley, but you can't win them all. The mood was expressed by a traffic cop who was forced from his routine post because he was carrying only routine equipment, "Mother..."

I volunteered to go out again when we got reports that the police were about to gas the Washington Monument grounds, where our big rally had ended a few hours earlier. So out I went in the deputy mayor's car with a chauffeur and a White House aide. We were waved through the police lines just in time to watch the police start to move down from the little hill at the Washington Monument to clear the grounds.

A hundred police officers formed a skirmish line in the pitch dark. Police vans tailed them with their headlights on to provide lighting. It was like the scene from *War of the Worlds* when the glowing creatures march across the landscape against the powerless earthlings.

It's hard to evaluate the impact of the antiwar movement. Certainly, Senator McCarthy's campaign led directly to President Johnson's decision not to run for reelection. But when Senator Robert Kennedy joined the campaign and was assassinated, the Democratic standard bearer became Vice President Hubert Humphrey who was unable to distance himself from Johnson's Vietnam policies. The result was the election of Richard Nixon. The antiwar movement certainly helped to demonstrate the nation's impatience with the war in Vietnam, with the result being that Nixon withdrew all the American combat forces over the next three years.

I took several lessons from my experience in helping to organize antiwar activities. The first is that my desire to avoid the escalation of conflict allowed me to work productively with people I disagreed with such as the Nixon staff members in the "rumor center" and the Civil Disturbance Unit of the DC police—but not the provocateur Abbie Hoffman. I also learned that the Moratorium leadership came together so quickly and worked so effectively because it was able to draw heavily on the personal relationships built during the presidential campaign of Senator McCarthy. I came to appreciate that I am more comfortable working behind the scenes rather than being the public face of a movement. And I came to appreciate that the high-pressure work that went into preparing for the huge march was gratifying and even fun because it was for a purpose I believed in, and especially because it was done with others who shared that purpose. The huge turnout for the event itself brought home to me that hundreds of thousands of people can be mobilized for coordinated activity. A final lesson: making a difference in the world requires patience for a sustained effort, a tolerance for ambiguity of results, and optimism that the effort may be worthwhile.

CHAPTER 18

TRYING TO REDUCE THE RISK OF WARS

Thus far, I've described my efforts outside the ivory tower to end war in Vietnam. The other activities I pursued were focused on reducing the risk of war, whether between the United States and its largest Cold War enemy, the Soviet Union, or preventing and reducing conflict in hot spots around the world. The experience of near catastrophe during the Cuban Missile Crisis led me to take a deep interest in reducing the risk of war. For example, my game theory work on cooperation was initially motivated by a search for ways in which two egoistic actors such as the United States and the Soviet Union could avoid conflict.

I always wanted to do more than just study international security affairs: I wanted to help make a difference, however small. As it happens, I have had five different endeavors in promoting international security that I've pursued over five decades:

working on arms control with the Soviet Union;
helping the United Nations peacekeeping efforts in the former Yugoslavia;
talking to leaders among the Israelis and Palestinians to explore how
to lessen the tensions between them;
helping to mediate a meeting of representatives from Iran, Saudi
Arabia, and Israel amid tensions; and
participating in semiofficial meetings with China and other countries on the military aspects of cyber stability.

Working on Arms Control with the Soviet Union

Because of my interest in international security, I've taken several opportunities over the years to visit the Soviet Union and then Russia. During my first visit, I attended the 1979 meeting of the International Political Science Association in Moscow with a side trip to Estonia. I was well aware of the tensions between the Russians and the Estonians and was curious to learn more about it. So I asked our hosts if they could arrange a meeting of local ethnic Russians and Estonians, but I was told it was impossible for them to even meet in the same room.

From 1985 to 1991, I served on a committee of American social scientists in the US National Academy of Sciences that worked with counterparts from the Soviet Academy of Sciences. The joint effort enlisted social scientists to promote joint or parallel research on important topics of mutual interest. At the first meeting, I drafted a memorandum of understanding outlining how the project would proceed over the next few years. When we met in Moscow at the Institute for the Study of the United States and Canada, the head of the Soviet delegation, Andrei Kokoshin, asked an aide to make sixteen copies for our consideration. The aide soon came back to say he couldn't do it without a signed statement from Kokoshin authorizing the use of the copying machine for this purpose. This struck me as a powerful indication of just how worried the Soviets were about any uncontrolled dissemination of information, even under glasnost, Gorbachev's campaign for openness. It is difficult to evaluate whether we accomplished much, although it was clear that the Soviet social scientists were as grateful for the interactions as we were.

At that first meeting in 1985, we were shown around several research institutes. Our visit to the Mathematical Economics Institute was followed that evening by a somewhat surreal experience shared by myself and Herb Simon, the chair of our delegation. The two of us were led somewhat clandestinely to the apartment of a former member of that very institute who had been fired when he applied to emigrate to Israel. Once there, we met several dozen other refuseniks who had similarly been fired from the Mathematical Economics Institute. Together in the crowded apartment we had an intellectual meeting in which Herb and I presented items from our research, as did several of the refuseniks. They were grateful for our coming, and we were pleased to be able to show our support. I learned that for people who are isolated like these refuseniks, even a little supportive attention can be very meaningful to all parties.

The late 1980s was a time near the end of the Cold War when President Gorbachev was trying to introduce a measure of democracy to the Soviet Union. Andrei Kokoshin told me that even very sophisticated Soviet intellectuals had only a limited sense of how democracy worked, and he invited me to write an article for his journal. The idea was to provide a Soviet audience with information about what it takes, according to Western political scientists, for democracy to work. Since the Soviets were already familiar with a strong executive, I wrote about what is needed to build a strong legislature. The paper was published in Russian in a leading Moscow journal.[2] Andrei was particularly struck by my saying that a premise of Western democracy is that people are not angels, so institutions should be structured such that when people respond to the incentives presented to them, the outcome will be acceptable. The premise that people are not angels was in sharp contrast with the discredited Soviet perspective that people are so malleable that they can be molded into eager supporters of communism.

The other activity with the Soviets was an initiative on the future of arms control organized by the US National Academy of Sciences and the Soviet Academy of Sciences. I was able to join because I had been elected to the National Academy of Sciences. And I felt free to devote the necessary time to the effort because, as I described in an earlier chapter, the MacArthur Prize gave me substantial time off from teaching. The American side was called the Committee for International Security and Arms Control (CISAC). Our delegation was headed by Pief Panofsky, former director of the Stanford Linear Accelerator Center. The delegation also included a recently retired head of the Joint Chiefs of Staff as well as a Nobel Laureate physicist. The Soviet counterpart committee included high-level scientists and retired generals. The purpose was to address technical and potentially sensitive issues in international security and arms control that our governments were not yet ready to address. Together these efforts helped Gorbachev develop his *perestroika* ("new thinking") that was instrumental in ending the Cold War.[3] Among the things I came to appreciate was how different the Soviet conception of nuclear deterrence was from the American conception. A striking piece of advice came from a retired Soviet general when we were discussing the value of an agreed-upon prohibition against attacking nuclear reactors in war. His advice was to put it in a treaty. He explained that if it were a mere statement of agreement by the two governments, the Soviet military would take it as advice that they were free to ignore. But if it were in a treaty, they would feel obliged to respect it.

The most amusing episode came when the bus carrying our delegations broke down on a highway in Kazakhstan. Out poured some of the world's leading scientists to help the driver figure out how to get the engine working again. None of them could. But someone spotted a traveling circus set up nearby and went to borrow a bus. We all agreed: "A political solution was better than a technical solution."

In this dialogue, I once suggested that our two delegations organize a war game among ourselves to learn more about how we interpret events and how they might react to a hypothetical crisis. Gen. David C. Jones, the recently retired chair of the Joint Chiefs of Staff, liked the idea, but no one else evinced much enthusiasm, so I let the idea drop.

After the meeting in Kazakhstan, the US side invited the Soviets to meet in Omaha at the headquarters of the Strategic Air Command, the organization in charge of the nuclear missiles that could destroy the Soviet Union. After the meeting, the two delegations toured the headquarters museum. I was pleased to take it all in at the side of Dick Garwin, who had been called by another physicist the only true genius he had ever met. When we got to the mock-up of the first H-bomb that was designed to be small enough for an airplane to carry, Dick Garwin turned to me and said proudly of the design, "That's me."

In 2002, I was invited to attend a small seminar in Moscow organized by one of Russia's wealthiest men, Mikhail Borisovich Khodorkovsky, the owner of Yukos, the Siberian oil company. The purpose of the seminar was for European and American intellectuals to exchange perspectives on how societies should be governed. Khodorkovsky was willing to challenge Vladimir Putin, the president of Russia, by promoting law-based government. The seminar included intellectuals from western Europe as well as the United States and Russia. When it ended, our travel expenses were reimbursed by a young man from an attaché case packed full of crisp

$100 bills and other hard currency. It felt like a scene out of a heist movie. I'm not sure whether we had any useful insights, but the effort came to an abrupt stop when Khodorkovsky was arrested the next year.

The evening before the start of the seminar, Russian TV reported that 979 people were being held hostage by about fifty Chechen separatists at a theater just a few miles away. They had enough explosives to bring down the roof of the theater, killing everyone inside. While it was going on, several self-appointed individuals tried to negotiate, apparently to no avail. At the seminar, I was approached by a reporter who used a word I had never heard before, saying, "You're a conflictologist. Would you to be willing to be interviewed by Ukrainian television about what's going on?" I agreed, expecting to be brought to a television studio. Instead, I was brought to the theater itself, which was surrounded by huge fire trucks as well as numerous police and paramilitary vehicles—a scary scene. I was ushered into a press room at the back of the building. In the interview, I had little to offer, except that talking is better than fighting.

A few hours later, Russian special forces raided the theater after dispersing a gas that was designed to put everyone to sleep. The result was that all the hostage takers were killed by the raiders, but about 125 of the hostages died from the gas. At the seminar, the Russians and the Americans heard the same reports but had completely different attitudes about whether the raid had been a success. The Americans' attitude was dominated by the death of so many of the hostages. The Russians, however, were pleased and even proud of the result, in which 85 percent of the hostages had escaped with their lives. It was a vivid example of how the same event can have very different meanings depending on one's perspective.

Helping UN Peacekeeping in the Former Yugoslavia

In the early 1990s, the breakup of Yugoslavia led to complex and vicious wars between Bosnians, Serbs, Croats, and other constituents of the former Yugoslavia. The UN sent peacekeepers to separate the parties, but the wars raged on and threatened to escalate further. In June 1995, I received an invitation from the United Nations peacekeeping forces to take part in a meeting in Vienna that would bring together two dozen participants that would include influential people from most of the warring parties. The idea was to foster new ways of thinking about the conflict. To make the discussion productive, none of them would be government officials. Also to be included were academics such as myself, observers from non-governmental organizations, and a few diplomats from other countries. The invitation warned me, "Some of the nicest people you would ever meet on all sides are killing and maiming each other mercilessly. It is quite difficult, even in conversations over dinner to get players on all sides to evolve from zero-sum thinking to mixed-sum calculations—not just in principle but in practice."

I was pleasantly surprised that the participants from the warring parties were able to be civil to each other, and even listen to each other.

In my own presentation, I explained the two-player Prisoner's Dilemma, and I emphasized that when interactions between parties are expected to continue over time, participants encounter what I called "the shadow of the future" that makes conditional cooperation based on reciprocity an effective strategy to use. The shadow of the future was relevant in the context of the breakup of Yugoslavia, I said, because the successors of the former Yugoslavia would be interacting with each other in war or peace for a long time to come. Among the very challenging questions I got in response: "You are assuming the players have equal power and can't be annihilated—but what if that's not true?" I didn't have a good answer at the time, but it struck me that this was a very good question, and so in the year that followed, I was inspired to work on models of attrition in which annihilation is possible. But I couldn't come up with anything better than the attrition models that had already been developed by economists for the study of price wars and other forms of oligopolistic competition.

Another good question was the following: "You are assuming only two players, but we have to deal with seven local players and five international players interacting at the same time—so what do you have to say about that?" Again, I had to admit that I didn't have a good answer, but when I went home I tried to see what my earlier work on norms might have to offer.[4]

All in all, it was a humbling experience. But it was also exhilarating to take part in a United Nations effort to bring people together whose countries were in the midst of war with each other, and to see that they could be civil with each other and even listen to each other. I also learned that even in the midst of conflict people can constructively engage in conversations with each other, and with academics like me who brought new ideas. Their criticisms of my game theoretic ideas about the Prisoner's Dilemma were very helpful to me in two regards. They showed that my work can be taken seriously by nonacademics even in the context of violent conflict, and that engaging with nonacademics could alert me to aspects of real conflict that I should try to incorporate in my future research to make it more relevant to promoting cooperation in real contexts.

Seeking Better Understanding between Israelis and the Palestinians

Since my teenage years, my Jewish upbringing gave me an interest in the Middle East and especially Israel. Decades later, I got personally involved in Middle East problems at the invitation of Scott Atran, a cultural anthropologist and a long-time friend from the University of Michigan. Scott has many interests, including the motivation and recruitment of terrorists and the importance of sacred values that can cause people to act in ways very different from what a weighing of costs and benefits would predict. Scott is also well known for field work in dangerous places, as well as academic collaborations.

His invitation was to attend a workshop in Sicily sponsored by a little-known Italian organization called the World Federation of Scientists. That gave the impetus to our plan to visit Israel and its neighbors in February 2007 and talk to leaders about how to make progress on the seemingly intractable problems between Israel and Palestine. Joining us on this and later trips to the Middle East was Rich Davis, who had worked on terrorism in the National Security Council. Working under the auspices of the World Federation of Scientists was useful because it suggested scientific credentials and didn't label us as representatives of any country, media outlet, political party, or lobbying group.

Our goal on these trips to the Middle East was to talk to all parties involved in the conflict, including Hamas, to gain insight into how to further advance scientific understanding of cultural and political conflict. The goal was to create new theoretical and practical frameworks for negotiation and cooperation.

When word reached the White House that we were planning to talk to senior people in Hamas whose charter called for the destruction of Israel, we heard from President George W. Bush's Middle East advisor at the National Security Council, Eliot Abrams. Mr. Abrams warned us that if we did talk to Hamas, we would lose our life savings because he would sue us for giving aid and comfort to terrorists. He explained that he couldn't win the suit, but our lawyers' fees would eat up everything we had. Scott had a terrific response which was, "How about if we brief you afterwards?" Since US officials weren't allowed to talk to Hamas leaders, this was a chance to get an inside look at how Hamas was thinking, or at least how they presented themselves outside of the public eye. So Abrams relented, and after our trip, as promised, we went to the White House to relate what we had heard.

What we had heard from the deputy head of the political bureau of Hamas, Mousa Marzook, was that if Israel withdrew to its 1967 borders and allowed a Palestinian state to form, there could be peace. He also said that in the interim, Hamas was looking for a *hudna*: a truce. But then, a hard-liner from the younger generation, Osama Hamdan, having no compunctions about disagreeing with his elder in front of us foreigners, said, "No, there *will* be war." I was surprised that one member of Hamas would so directly contradict another in front of us foreigners. This suggested to me that there might be deep divisions within the organization, and that those divisions might well include a generational divide between some older members who might be open to compromise and some younger members who wouldn't be.

To prepare for these meetings, l learned about Palestinian narratives. Having been brought up on Zionist narratives, I had to work hard to hold in my head two emotionally powerful but inconsistent versions of history, and it wasn't easy.

We also went to hear from several members of Hamas who had been elected to the Palestinian legislature. As we were leaving, one person put her hand on her heart, bowed her head, and gave me an appreciative smile. It brought home to me that sometimes just being listened to can be meaningful.

On our next trip to the Middle East, in December 2009, we met the foreign minister of Syria, Walid Muallem, who explained his step-by-step plan to normalize relations with Israel based on their withdrawal from the Golan Heights. We asked about Israel's demand that they control the shoreline of the Sea of Galilee, the source of much of their fresh water. He explained that the president of Syria, Bashar al-Assad, had swum there as a child and was unwilling to give it up. I couldn't tell if this sentimental story was to be taken seriously, but in any case it was clear that access to the Sea of Galilee was important to Syria, probably because they wanted to retain the ability to at least threaten Israel's water supply.

We also met the leader of Hamas, Khaled Mashal. He turned out to be charismatic in a way that reminded me of President John Kennedy. At the meeting, Scott Atran asked him, "In your heart, do [you] feel that peace—salaam—with Israel is possible? . . . be as sincere as you can, personally." According to his own aides, Mr. Mashal was surprised by the question, and they were surprised by his answer, which they supposedly had never heard before: "The heart is different from the mind, and the mind resists by all logic, but the heart says 'yes.' In my heart, I feel peace—salaam—with Israel is possible. But when we have a balance of power."

We also went to the headquarters of another terrorist organization hosted in Damascus, the Palestinian Islamic Jihad. Their leader, Ramadan Shalah, told us that the two-state solution was dead because of the expansion of Jewish settlements in the West Bank. He also disagreed with Hamas's idea of a long-term hudna with Israel because Israel would only use the time to make things worse. To make himself very clear, he added that "I will never, under any conditions, accept the existence of the state of Israel."

When we got back to the States, we found out that Ramadan Shalah was on the FBI's Most Wanted List with a $5 million reward on his head, so I immediately reported our contact with him to the State Department and the FBI. I even filled out the FBI online tip form, but it took three weeks for them to even get back to me. When they did, I said that I had already entered everything I knew about him so there was no point in an interview. The agent from the FBI told me she was disappointed because she was looking forward to talking with me.

While still in Damascus, a third terrorist organization, perhaps the most radical of all, the Popular Front for the Liberation of Palestine, heard we were in town speaking to the others, and they wanted to have us come to talk to them too. So we did. It wasn't very productive. Their leaders, the décor of their office, and their speech seemed like it was taken from an old Bolshevik movie, complete with leather caps and a bust of Lenin. We didn't hear anything new, and they were not interested in our perspective.

We also spoke to high-level people in the West Bank's Palestinian Authority, political leaders in Israel, and people at the US Embassy in Tel Aviv. Once, a Palestinian leader shared an opinion with us and immediately stopped himself and said, "If it ever gets out that I said that, I could be killed." His remark was reminiscent of the assassination of the king of Jordan in 1951 when there were rumors that he had been talking with Israel about a separate peace. I silently wondered why a Palestinian leader would say something to us that was potentially lethal to him. Indeed, it happened a second time, when someone from another country stopped himself after sharing and said, "If it gets out that I said that it would be the end of my career." In both cases, we had met the person only ten minutes earlier. I was amazed at the level of trust that we were offered. I believe that Scott's training as an anthropologist and his warm personality were crucial to making people feel at ease with him. Another factor was that we were not journalists looking for a story to publish, or people with an axe to grind. Even so, the trust we received was remarkable.

In Israel, our host was retired general Itzik Ben-Israel, the one who had found my model of the rational timing of surprise to be so useful during the 1982 Lebanon War. After showing us around Tel Aviv and introducing us to various officials, he asked me what I'd like to do on our last day in Israel. I said I'd like to meet with the prime minister, known to all as "Bibi" Netanyahu. Sure enough, Itzik set up a meeting for us the next day. Bibi told me that he had read my book on cooperation, "but we're not ready for that yet." After we discussed Israel-Palestinian problems, Bibi asked us what could be done to stop Iran from getting a nuclear weapon. We didn't have anything much to offer. After the meeting was over, two of Bibi's aides stayed behind to ask again, saying they were *really* interested in new ideas to stop Iran from getting the bomb. Again, we came up blank. Little did we know that Stuxnet malware was already being deployed by Israel and the United States to disrupt Iran's production of fuel for a nuclear weapon—a fact that did not become public until six months later. But Stuxnet was never completely effective, so the question was still very much alive for the Israeli leadership when we met them.

The next year, Scott Atran, Richard Davis, and I went back to the Middle East to explore the possibilities for alleviating the water shortage that was the basis of so much rivalry in the region. One idea that intrigued us was the possibility of building a canal from the Red Sea at the southern tip of Israel to the Dead Sea between the Israeli-occupied West Bank and Jordan. The idea was that the Red Sea was at sea level, and the Dead Sea was about 1,500 feet below sea level, the lowest point on the surface of the earth. With a vertical drop of about eight times the height of the Niagara Falls, the project had huge potential to generate electricity for many purposes, including desalinization. We spoke to Israeli and Palestinian water experts and learned about the range of environmental and economic problems involved. Unfortunately, the leading Palestinian expert told us that while the project might be feasible, he was against it. He said it would just play into Israel's scheme to promote the economy of the West Bank to make the occupation tolerable. For us, it was quite a disappointment. More than a decade later, the Red-Dead canal is still under active consideration, but construction has not begun.

Later, when a massive uprising overthrew the repressive regime of Hosni Mubarak, we decided to go to Cairo to learn what we could about the new government run by the Muslim Brotherhood under Mohamed Morsi. One of the people we interviewed was Safwat Hegazi, the very person who had led the process leading to the selection of Morsi. Safwat Hegazi was a religious teacher and well-known TV preacher who ranted against Jews and advocated for the destruction of Israel. Not being shy, I mentioned that we had seen a book for sale on the streets of Cairo—*The Protocols of the Elders of Zion*—that described a meeting of Jews to plot a world takeover. He said he was not only familiar with it, but he taught it at the university. When asked if he knew it was a czarist forgery, he said, "It doesn't matter. It's true." Our conversation didn't get very far beyond that, although we did have a nice photo to remember the event.

Figure 5. Rich Davis, me, Scott Atran, and Safwat Hegazi in Cairo, October 2012

Exploring the Differences between Iran, Saudi Arabia, and Israel

I had a chance to meet Mahmoud Ahmadinejad, Iran's bellicose president, when he came to New York in 2011 to give a speech at the United Nations. Before the speech, he invited about fifteen Middle East and international security specialists to exchange views with him. I accepted partly out of curiosity and partly to have a chance to speak to him. He began the meeting with a statement about how America's relations with Iran needed to be based on justice if peace were to be attained. He explained that each person could make a statement and then he would then respond. After we spoke, he paraphrased each person's contribution and asked if he had understood it correctly before giving his own view. I was impressed with how accurately he was able to recount views he disagreed with. When my turn came, I simply said, "It is hard to believe you really want peace when you deny the Holocaust." I remember his response well. First, he

said, we hadn't attained peace *before* we started talking about the Holocaust, implying that ending his Holocaust denial wouldn't bring peace
either. It was a good debater's point but hardly relevant. Then he added
that most people who bring up his denial of the Holocaust don't care at
all about the Holocaust, but just want to attack Iran. I was angry with the
implication that I didn't care about the Holocaust since if my grandpar-
ents hadn't left eastern Europe in time they and my parents would not
have survived. Although I didn't get a chance to say that, at least I did
have the chance to object to his denial of the Holocaust. He invited me
to visit Iran, but I never took him up on the offer. Only later did I realize
that he wasn't interested in hearing what we had to say. He only wanted
practice in sharpening his responses to critics.

In July 2015, the United States and Iran signed a deal to prevent Iran
from obtaining nuclear weapons in return for the removal of UN sanctions. Known formally as the Joint Comprehensive Plan of Action, the
deal was supported by the five permanent members of the UN Security
Council, as well as the European Union. However, there was still concern that other countries in the region, such as Saudi Arabia, Egypt, or
Turkey, might seek nuclear weapons. To explore these issues of nuclear
proliferation, Scott Atran developed an audacious plan to get representatives of Israel, Iran, and Saudi Arabia to sit down together for several
days of informal discussions. The venue would be Oxford University's
new Centre for the Resolution of Intractable Conflict. The name of the
center struck me as a bit odd, but the center's location in Britain, as well
as its affiliation with Oxford, was helpful. Also helpful was the recruitment of John Alderdice, Speaker of the Northern Ireland parliament,
to be the moderator. He was well known for his major role in achieving
peace between the Protestants and Catholics in Northern Ireland—work
that led to his becoming Lord John Alderdice.

Scott Atran and Lord Alderdice were able to recruit an influential Iranian from a leading think tank in Tehran, as well as a close advisor to one
of the leading princes in Saudi Arabia. We were also able to recruit Itzik
Ben-Israel, who had used my work on the rational timing of surprise and
who was still an important advisor to the Israeli government. I was grateful to be included along with a few other academics and advisors. I gave
a short talk on the problem of potential spoilers in an agreement, using

the example of the Oslo Peace Accords between Israel and the Palestinian Liberation Organization that was undermined by spoilers, including
terrorist attacks by Hamas.

The discussions between the Israeli, Saudi, and Iranian participants
were quite helpful, having a tenor that was both civil and candid. I felt
useful when I was able to de-escalate the one and only shouting match,
an angry debate between the Iranian and the Israeli over whether Israel
had a right to attain nuclear weapons. I intervened and pointed out that
that issue need not be resolved in order for us to make progress on understanding each other's perspectives on the other matters at hand.

The most useful thing to come out of the meeting was an appreciation of how fragile the Iranian nuclear deal was due to the lack of any
visible improvement in the lives of Iranians, which had been anticipated with the lifting of the UN sanctions. One of the reasons for the
lack of improvement in the Iranian economy was the reluctance of European firms and other prospective investors to take up the opportunities
offered by the end of the UN sanctions. We learned at the meeting that
the reluctance of these potential investors was due to their uncertainty
about what would get them in trouble for violating the remaining US
sanctions against state-sponsored terrorism and the Iranian ballistic missile program.

After the meeting, I pondered how to prevent the Iranians from giving up on the nuclear deal because they weren't seeing its expected benefits. I realized that a useful step would be for the US to clarify what sorts
of investments in Iran would be acceptable, and what sorts the US would
regard as violations of its own remaining sanctions. I found the lengthy
U.S. Treasury Department policy statement online, but I couldn't make
much sense of it. I realized that part of my problem was that I wasn't
familiar with the legal and business language of the document. But I also
thought that its opaqueness might, in fact, be deliberate. Fortunately, a
colleague of mine at the Ford School, John Ciorciari, had worked in the
Treasury Department several years earlier. He knew the author of the
document I was struggling with and put me in touch with him. I sent
an email explaining why I thought it would be important to clarify what
was and was not acceptable to the US government for investment in Iran
to sustain Iran's acceptance of the nuclear deal. The response I got was

carefully worded, but I understood it to mean that the obscurity of US policy was deliberate. I inferred that the Treasury Department was concerned that if it clarified what investment in Iran was permissible, Congress might prevent *any* kind of investing in Iran—and that would *really* place the nuclear deal in jeopardy.

The idea I came up with to deal with this problem was to submit an op-ed to the *New York Times* explaining the problem and recommending that the Treasury Department clarify its policy on what kinds of investments would trigger the remaining US sanctions, and what kinds would be permissible. The *Times* didn't publish it, although soon thereafter they did report European and Iranian complaints that the nuclear deal was in jeopardy because of ambiguity in US trade policy.

Reducing the Risk of Cyber Conflict with China and Others

My interest in China stems from two sources, both originating in college. At the University of Chicago, I took a yearlong course on Chinese civilization. I became fascinated by how sophisticated the Chinese civilization was in its early technology, but also by how it was often able to sustain a unitary government over populations that dwarfed European principalities and even nation-states. In addition to my enduring interest in Chinese civilization, the Cuban Missile Crisis led me to a PhD in political science with a specialization in international security issues among the great powers.

I first went to China in 2006 as the leader of a delegation of American political scientists. When meeting our counterparts in Beijing and Shanghai, I asked what the hardest thing was for them to understand about America. In both places, my interlocutors had the same single-word answer: "religion." They couldn't understand whether an American leader who invoked religion as a justification for policy was simply pandering to his or her constituents, or whether religion actually guided policy. I thought it was a very good question, and I didn't have an answer.

In preparation for our visit, I asked our hosts to take us to a remote village off the beaten tourist paths. They obliged, and we knew it was indeed off the tourist paths because, while there, we saw workers peeking at us from behind trees. I'd heard that the Chinese government had announced that in the previous year there had been over 100,000 protest demonstrations. I asked about this surprising number. The village leaders explained that such protests served the useful function of alerting the regional party leaders of a local problem. The higher-ups could then investigate and even discipline any local officials whose misbehavior might have justified the protest. I realized that far from being protests against the Communist regime, they often led to appreciation for the regime for being responsive to local problems.

While in southern China, I asked our local guide whether people there were still afraid of Japan. She replied, "We're not afraid of Japan, we just hate them." This response brought home to me how durable hatred can be, but it also reminded me of the example of how France and Germany were able to overcome their hostility from World War II by working together in NATO against the common threat of the Soviet Union.

About this time, there was a great deal of attention to Chinese use of cyber tools to steal American technology. That got me to thinking about extending my earlier work on the rational timing of surprise to analyze the rational timing of surprise in a military context: specifically, cyber warfare. The analogy to a new secret weapon would be a zero-day exploit—a cyber tool that has never been used before. The mathematical model could be quite similar to the one I developed for rational timing of deception because the cases both embodied the problem of when to use a resource for surprise, knowing that if you wait too long for a high-stakes opportunity, the weapon or tool might be discovered and rendered less effective before you have a chance to exploit its potential. Working with my postdoctoral fellow, Rumen Iliev, we applied my work on the rational timing of surprise to the domain of cyber weapons.[5] The resulting paper received widespread attention including in *Science*, *Nature*, *ArsTechnica*, and the BBC World News Service. For example, the *Science* commentary called it "a solid logical foundation for fresh thinking in the cyber security field." The work was also reviewed in Chinese and Russian media, occasionally with the suggestion that, perhaps, the authors were planning a new war.

After the publication of the cyber paper, I was asked by the US Cyber Command on behalf of its director, General Keith Alexander, to develop analogies to cyber conflict. He had previously tried using the Pearl Harbor analogy to warn the public about the danger of a massive surprise attack with cyber weapons, but that analogy did not achieve much credence. So he called a meeting of about a dozen outsiders to work on other potential analogies to cyber conflict. I had fun with the exercise, coming up with thirty-five analogies and the lessons that each could provide.[6]

General Alexander then invited me to a private briefing to discuss these analogies and to brief him about the rational timing of surprise in a cyber context. Two of my analogies were particularly interesting to him. The Battle of Britain in 1940 between the air forces of Britain and Germany demonstrated that a major campaign could be fought in just one domain and suggested that the same might be true for a major conflict involving just cyber weapons. The other analogy that caught his attention was the demonstration that industrial sabotage by means of malware was nothing new. In 1982, the CIA introduced malware into software for pipeline control that was exported from Canada and installed by the Soviet Union in Siberia, leading to "the most monumental non-nuclear explosion and fire ever seen from space."[7]

Once I had started thinking seriously about cyber conflict, I realized that game theory could help illuminate the difficulty of attribution of a cyber attack. I began working once more with Stephanie Forrest, and we were joined by two of our graduate students, Benjamin Edwards and Alexander Furnas. We published a strategic analysis of whether or not to accuse someone of an attack, which we called the "blame game."[8] We showed how the best strategic choice for the victim depends on the vulnerability of the attacker, the knowledge level of the victim, payoffs for different outcomes, and the beliefs of each player about their opponent. We were able to specify the conditions under which peace (i.e., no attacks) is stable, when attacks should be tolerated, the consequences of asymmetric technical attribution capabilities, and when a mischievous third party or an accident can undermine peace.

While working on issues of cyber conflict, it struck me that many of the contributors to the field were either "techies" who focused on issues of computer security or political scientists who focused on issues of international security. But there were very few people who had a good understanding of both sides of the problem. So I started a course at the University of Michigan on cyber conflict that brought together graduate students from the Ford School of Public Policy, law students, and computer scientists from the College of Engineering. To promote lateral learning, I arranged for them to do group projects in which each group would include students from both public policy and computer science. It was a small step, but perhaps it would help bridge the gap between the two disciplines so that they could at least appreciate what the other had to offer in the analysis of cyber conflict.

One of the main issues in cyber conflict is the risk of instability should cyber weapons be used by nations or other actors against each other. For example, cyber weapons might have the potential to disrupt nuclear command and control facilities, thereby potentially weakening the deterrent value of a secure second strike that major nations have been relying on for decades to attain stability. The United States, Russia, and China all understood this problem. Everyone also understood that it would be impossible to undertake traditional arms-control measures, since it was not possible to verify any prohibition on the development or production of cyber weapons. Perhaps the best that could be hoped for would be the development of widely accepted norms about cyber conflict.

There are several international venues for working on these issues. The one I participated in is called the Roundtable on Military Aspects of Cyber Security. The most active participants have been the Americans and the Chinese, although Russia and a half dozen other countries have also taken part. The meetings were set up as a so-called Track 1.5 process. A Track 1 process involves officials, such as meetings of foreign ministers. A Track 2 process, such as the one with the Soviets I had taken part in earlier, involves only people *not* in government, such as academics, former officials, and retired military officers. The Track 1.5 process of the Roundtable involves government employees, but not policymakers. For example, it includes people from the national defense universities of both the US and China, institutions set up to train future military leaders and help develop military doctrine.

At one meeting in Shanghai, I made a presentation on how to de-escalate a cyber conflict.[9] I pointed out that the Chinese had twice shut down their hotline with the US in times of crisis. I made the point that this is precisely when a hotline might be most needed. Immediately afterward, the head of the Chinese delegation, Lu Chuanying, took me aside to say—I remember his words exactly—"It may be a cultural thing, but when someone insults you, you don't want to talk to them." I took him to mean that the Chinese had felt insulted by the United States, and they didn't want to respond in kind. I couldn't think of a good reply at the time, but I later thought that not wanting to talk to someone who insulted you is not just specific to a single culture. In fact, it may be nearly universal. So the lesson I took is to be careful to avoid insulting the other side if you want to be able to de-escalate.

I later heard about a good example of just how hard it can be to avoid even unintentional insults. When China tested rockets that landed near Taiwan in 1996, the United States sent the aircraft carrier USS Independence toward the Taiwan Straits to show how seriously we took China's action. To our surprise, the Chinese took it as a deliberate insult because they thought that the name of the chosen ship signaled support for the independence of Taiwan, a hugely sensitive issue for them. No doubt the US didn't choose that particular ship based on its name, but merely because it was in the general area at the time.

At a later meeting, I gave a presentation expressing my concern that it may be hard for the US (as a status quo power) and China (as a rising power) to work things out between them. This got a mixed reception: the Chinese participants said that they discussed this issue a lot, but several Americans thought the historical cases employed to support the concern were not similar enough to the relationship between the United States and China to be compelling.

I can't say that the roundtable made much progress on developing norms to reduce the risk of instability in cyber conflict in the four years of my participation. But we did make progress on our secondary objectives of learning each other's terminology to avoid some potential misunderstandings, getting a glimpse into how the Chinese and American governments are organized differently to deal with both the political and the military aspects of cyber issues, and developing personal relationships that could be useful in the future.

A Year at the State Department

In 2014, it had been almost fifty years since I had worked inside the government as a summer intern in the Pentagon. So I decided to take another look, this time at the State Department. Stephanie Forrest told me about a program at the State Department to bring in scientists for a year. Although the program usually drew ecologists, chemists, public health doctors, and the like, I figured they might take a political scientist too.

I was concerned that my having interviewed terrorists might prevent me from getting the necessary security clearance. I had been quite transparent about that, even publishing an op-ed piece with Scott Atran in the *New York Times* on "Why We Talk to Terrorists."[10] As required, I filled out the forms, including the requirement to name every foreign contact I had in the last seven years. This was followed by the routine interview with an FBI contractor. The interviewer looked the forms over and asked me who this "Khalid Mashal" was. I said, "If you look down two lines, you will see he's the head of Hamas." He calmly said, "Oh," and went on. Below this was a list based on business cards I had collected from the thirty or so Chinese academics I met while leading a tour of American political scientists to China several years earlier. He noted that I had provided each contact's full title, office address, and phone number. He said, "You get an A+! I've never seen anything so thorough."

While waiting for the security clearance, I went to the State Department to meet people who might want to have me in their office for a year. Since I had a long-term interest in international security affairs, I met with the admiral who had been assigned by the navy to work at the State Department on political-military affairs. He told me that when he served at a naval base, he'd had a thousand people working for him, but at the State Department, he had only five. I felt a little sorry for him. Although my clearance hadn't come through yet, he was able to give me an example of what he was working on. The question was what countries the United States should sell weaponized drones to. He said that his office had been working with the Defense Department for almost two years on this policy question, and he was expecting that they'd have an answer soon. I decided that since I didn't enjoy watching paint dry, I probably wouldn't enjoy working in that office either.

I heard about another possible placement that sounded a lot more promising. This would be with David Thorne, who was a special advisor to the secretary of state, John Kerry. Mr. Thorne was an old friend of Secretary Kerry's, having known him since the time they were members of the elite Skull and Bones Society as undergraduates at Yale. They had been close ever since. In fact, when Secretary Kerry completed the arduous process of negotiating the nuclear deal with Iran, he and his wife went on a Caribbean vacation with Thorne and his wife. They were that close. So I figured I couldn't do better than a placement in which there was only one person between myself and the secretary of state.

Mr. Thorne and I hit it off, and I accepted his invitation to join his small staff working on the theme of promoting "shared prosperity" between the United States and other countries. My interests were not mainly in economic relations, but I thought it was too good an opportunity to pass up. Only later did I realize how naïve I was. First of all, my aspiration to be a fly on the wall at high-level meetings proved impossible because those kinds of meetings require a lot of trust between the participants, and the last thing they wanted was a stranger present. The other thing I learned is that the Economic Bureau of the State Department had the authority to make economic policy at the State Department and a special advisor was, in effect, a fifth wheel.

Fortunately, talking to terrorists did not prevent me from attaining the trust of the US government. I did finally get a security clearance, though not before I had already been working at the State Department for three months. (Getting the clearance meant that I no longer had to be escorted to the bathroom.)

I tried to be helpful to Mr. Thorne, but eventually it became clear that he didn't know what to do with me, and I didn't know what to do with him. But I did try. For example, I came up with an idea to improve the personnel rating system for foreign service officers. I had great respect for the dedication and skill of these career diplomats, and I soon realized that the department encouraged good performance by promoting the most successful personnel sooner rather than later. I was interested in how the evaluation was done and whether it might be improved. Thorne told me the name of the person who was working on exactly that and encouraged me to "get in the weeds" (as he called it) to work on the problem. So I went to the person who had recently been tasked with improving the rating system, and he listened respectfully to my idea.

The idea was intended to be an improvement on the standard method of soliciting an evaluation from an officer's superior at his or her most recent assignment. My idea was that it would also be helpful also to ask the officer's supervisors from several years earlier whether the candidate for promotion had started anything of lasting value. For example, if the candidate reported that she was proud of a project she had started in Athens five years earlier, it would be helpful to know from the current person in charge at Athens whether that project had flourished since then or had left no trace. All it would take would be an hour of time from the Athens personnel to write a brief report, as well as an extra page to read in the candidate's evaluation folder. I said there were two potential gains: first, it would help distinguish who was really deserving of promotion, and second, it would encourage officers to build things of lasting value rather than just being concerned with the short-run perspective of their current supervisor. When I was finished, my colleague said, simply, "No." He explained that his writ was to make the promotion process simpler, rather than better. Oh, well.

While I wasn't able to make much of a contribution to policy, I benefitted from talking to people and attending information meetings. For example, I went to a one-day seminar that explained the distinct roles of the seventeen agencies that make up the intelligence community, from the well-known CIA to the more obscure organization called the National Geospatial-Intelligence Agency. One talk was given by the director of the National Intelligence Council, the small organization that gathers information from all sources and writes the authoritative assessments of mid- and long-term strategic questions.

The director started with the sensible point that the intelligence community shouldn't be expected to give precise and accurate predictions about specifics such as the exact day when and place where the Arab Spring would begin. But he then went on to say something silly: the US Weather Service spends a billion dollars a year and even they can't predict tomorrow's weather any better than saying it will be exactly the same as today's weather. I didn't think that could be right, since if it's clear today, and the Weather Service predicts a 90 percent chance of rain tomorrow, then it will probably rain. I tried coming up afterward to suggest that he shouldn't make such an obviously incorrect statement since it will make him look like he is either careless or foolish. I knew he'd likely make the same point about weather prediction in the future, since he had it projected on his opening slide. But he left quickly, and I didn't get the chance. Afterward I thought of emailing him my suggestion, but I was hesitant. Would it be better if he were saved from later embarrassment, or would it be better if later audiences found out that there was a reason to take anything else he said with a grain of salt? What would you do? (Spoiler alert: see the endnote for what I did).[11]

CHAPTER 19

COUNTERING HOSTILE INFLUENCE

Starting in 2019, I worked with Scott Atran, Richard Davis, and Hasan Davulcu on a State Department contract to better understand hostile influence campaigns on social media, such as those being conducted by Russia. Our work was based on the premise that state-sponsored hostile influence campaigns are instruments of national power that use social media to mislead audiences or falsely report information in order to drive wedges within and between the populations of its adversaries, most notably the US and its allies. We were especially interested in understanding how maligning campaigns exploit psychological biases and political vulnerabilities in nations' sociocultural landscapes and among transnational and substate actors.

On May 20, 2020, Scott, Rich, and I were invited to brief the staff of the National Security Council on our findings so far. We met in the famous Situation Room, giving the briefing added gravitas. Among the dozen attendees were the deputy national security adviser, the National Security Council officer for Russia, and a representative from the Department of Homeland Security. My role had two parts. First I described the historical context of Soviet and Russian influence campaigns since World War II, noting that the goals of their media campaigns hadn't changed much with the advent of social media. They were still trying to polarize foreign societies to undermine the legitimacy of their governments, promote favored policies, and increase hostility toward the United States, especially among NATO countries. The second part of my presentation was a checklist of things to consider before selecting a response, including whether the response should be made public, whether it should be proportional to the current provocation, and (my old concern) whether hitherto secret capabilities should be employed on this occasion. Those present stayed well beyond the hour we were allocated. Afterward, one of the National Security Council participants said our presentation was "mega-useful."

Since then, I continued to work with Scott and Rich on issues related to hostile influence campaigns on social media. With the help of colleagues at Artis International, a research firm, we tested three hypotheses about what goes viral to see if we could get a better understanding of how hostile influence campaigns work.[12] For example, we found that negativity, causal arguments, and threats to target audiences' personal or societal core values tend to make messages spread widely on social media.

CONCLUDING THOUGHTS

CHAPTER 20

CROSSING THE MOAT

I've found it fruitful to cross the moat back and forth between the ivory tower and the outside world. My policy engagement has often been enabled by my academic work. For example, people from Israel to China were happy to meet with me because they had read *The Evolution of Cooperation*. My participation in arms control work with Soviet senior scientists and retired generals was made possible by my having been elected to the National Academy of Sciences, which in turn was made possible by my academic efforts. My meeting with the head of the Cyber Command was made possible by my work on the rational timing of surprise as well as my study of historical analogies. I was called upon to help the UN peacekeeping forces in the wars in the former Yugoslavia because of my game theory modeling. In addition, my academic work was used by policymakers themselves, as exemplified by the Israeli application of my model of the rational timing of surprise in the context of their conflict with Syria.

It has worked the other way too. My research and teaching have benefitted from my policy engagement. Among the research projects that were inspired by my policy engagement are the development and maintenance of norms, the possibility of overcoming seemingly intractable conflict by reframing the sacred issues at stake, the empirical study of hostile influence campaigns on social media, and even my collaboration with oncologists on practical problems of cancer therapy. Each of these avenues of inquiry opened up new directions for my research on the evolution of cooperation and bottom-up self-organization.

My policy engagements also brought home to me that my passion for cooperation was not always shared by both sides of a rivalry. This was most clear in the contrasting visions of the Palestinian terrorist groups we talked with about possibilities for their long-term relationship with Israel. While the leader of Hamas could envision living with Israel indefinitely, the leaders of the Palestinian Islamic Jihad and the Popular Front for the Liberation of Palestine could not. Another example was the Holocaust denial of the president of Iran, which suggested to me that he really didn't want to work things out with Israel. In terms of my research on the iterated Prisoner's Dilemma, I came to better appreciate that there was a fundamental difference between two kinds of rivalry. In one kind of rivalry both sides envision the importance of the shadow of the future caused by the prospect that the relationship will continue. In the other kind of rivalry one or both sides intend to destroy rather than live with the other. The trench warfare case is interesting in this regard because both types of rivalry were present. At the local level of German and Allied units facing each other in a static context, the live and let live system was mutually advantageous, but at the national level both sides were aiming to destroy the other.

I also came to better appreciate that my tendency to focus on two-sided relationships was more restrictive than I had hoped for. In the context of norms, I had already modeled the importance of third parties in enforcing a given norm not only by punishing violators but also by punishing those who don't punish the violators. Yet, when I came to work on establishing norms for preventing instability in cyber conflict with representatives for China, Russia, the United States, and others, I came to see that there was little prospect that we could develop candidates for cyber norms that would be enforced by third parties in a two-sided cyber conflict. And when I presented my findings to influential people from all sides of the fighting in the former Yugoslavia, they not only reminded me that some parties to the conflict wanted to destroy each other rather than reach an accommodation, but there were twelve rather than two sides to the conflict. These experiences and others reinforced my appreciation of the importance of understanding when and how whole populations of actors can sometimes achieve self-organization as in coalition formation that minimizes the strangeness of bedfellows or instead lurch toward a dangerous level of political polarization.

CHAPTER 21

LOOKING FORWARD

Of all my work, I think that the biggest impact has been to help people avoid the dangerous zero-sum fallacy: namely, the idea that whenever there is rivalry whatever is good for you is bad for me. The prevalence of the zero-sum fallacy is why it was so surprising that you can win a tournament without outdoing anyone you interact with.

Today, there is an alarming range of current and looming problems in the world. In no particular order these problems include climate change, food shortages, racism, subordination of women, war, threats to democracy in the United States and elsewhere, concentration of wealth, nuclear proliferation, weakening of the norms of international order, a deeply dissatisfied Russia, and an assertive China. I hope that my work on cooperation will help achieve progress on problems such as these.

ACKNOWLEDGMENTS

Gratitude is not only the greatest of all virtues,
but it is the parent of all the others.

—CICERO, AS QUOTED TO ME BY ROGER PORTER

Writing this autobiography made me realize that throughout my career I have not expressed often enough or fully enough the gratitude I feel. In a long career I've accumulated immense debts to many colleagues, students, relatives, and friends—too many to list. But I certainly want to point out that many of the recognitions I have received would not have been possible without the help of the collaborators I have mentioned throughout the book.

I am also grateful to the University of Michigan for having hired me when Berkeley turned me down for tenure. It was a difficult moment, to say the least. Michigan might well have decided that Berkeley knew me best and if *they* didn't think I was worthy, then why should Michigan take a chance on a lifelong commitment? But Michigan did, and I've always been grateful.

The Ford School and the Political Science Department at Michigan have been my professional homes for almost fifty years. I am grateful for the many ways I've been supported along the way. The long line of deans and chairs did so much to empower my work through the generosity of the resources they gave me, and their flexibility in teaching assignments. I appreciate, too, that no one ever pressured *me* to be a chair or a dean. Maybe everyone knew that I wasn't cut out for it. After all, I'm a lot better at candor than at tact. And so I'm grateful for those who did step up to the plate.

I am pleased to acknowledge the people who have read this book in draft form and gave valuable feedback: Padideh Aghanoury and Charles Anderson of Editing Press, Scott Atran, David Axelrod, Lily Axelrod, Vera Axelrod, Linda Brakel, Sara Fink, William Fink, Stephanie Forrest, Debbie Gilden, Daniel Hamermesh, Douglas Hofstadter, Dan Kleinman, Scott Page, Robert Putnam, Amy Saldinger, Ellen Schwartz, and Leigh Tesfatsion.

I owe a special debt to Douglas Hofstadter, one of the smartest, most versatile, creative, and generous people I know. He has not only been a huge booster of my work but also provided me with the encouragement necessary to complete this autobiography.

Above all, I want to thank Robert Putnam for a lifetime of friendship and enrichment. Bob is one of the world's leading political scientists. He is not only a great scholar who can find subtle patterns across diverse data sets, but his insights into how to build networks of trust and reciprocity have drawn the eager attention of hundreds of thousands of citizens as well as presidents and prime ministers. It has been a privilege to have him as a best friend, and a discerning critic.

NOTES

Part I

1. Saying that addition distributes over multiplication as well as vice versa means it is true not only that a*(b+c) = a*b + a*c, as in ordinary algebra, but in Boolean algebra also that a+(b*c) = (a+b)*(a+c), where "*" and "+" indicate the "and" and "or" operators, respectively.

2. Arthur Samuel, "Some Studies in Machine Learning Using the Game of Checkers," *IBM Journal of Research and Development* 3 (1959): 211–29. Reprinted (with minor additions and corrections) in *Computers and Thought*, ed. Edwin A. Feigenbaum and Julian Feldman (New York: McGraw-Hill, 1963).

3. Robert Axelrod, "Bureaucratic Decision Making in the Military Assistant Program: Some Empirical Findings," in *American Foreign Policy: A Bureaucratic Perspective*, ed. Morton Halperin and Arnold Kanter (New York: Little, Brown, 1973), 11–20.

4. R. Duncan Luce and Howard Raiffa, *Games and Decisions: Introduction and Critical Survey* (New York: Wiley & Sons, 1957).

5. C. E. Shannon, "A Mathematical Theory of Communication," *Bell Systems Technical Journal* 27 (July 1948): 379–423.

6. Robert Axelrod, "Conflict of Interest: An Axiomatic Approach," *Journal of Conflict Resolution* 11, no. 1 (1967): 87–99. See also Robert Axelrod, *Conflict of Interest: A Theory of Divergent Goals with Applications to Politics* (Chicago: Markham Publishing, 1970).

Part II

1. Elinor Ostrom, "Biography of Robert Axelrod," *PS: Political Science & Politics* 40, no. 1 (2007): 171–74.

2. Michael D. Cohen, James G. March, and Johan P. Olsen, "A Garbage Can Model of Organizational Choice," *Administrative Science Quarterly* 17, no. 1 (1972): 1–25.

3. Robert M. Axelrod and Michael D. Cohen. *Harnessing Complexity: Organizational Implications of a Scientific Frontier* (New York: Basic Books, 2001).

4. On-Line Guide for Newcomers to Agent-Based Modeling in the Social Sciences, http://www2.econ.iastate.edu/tesfatsi/abmread.htm

5 Elinor Ostrom, "Biography of Robert Axelrod," *PS: Political Science & Politics* 40, no. 1 (2007): 171–74.

6. Robert Axelrod, "Political Science and Beyond: Presidential Address to the American Political Science Association," *Perspectives on Politics* 6, no. 1 (2008): 3–9.

7. John H. Aldrich, ed., *Interdisciplinarity: Its Role in a Discipline-Based Academy* (Oxford: Oxford University Press, 2014).

Part III

1. R. Duncan Luce and Howard Raiffa, *Games and Decisions* (New York: Wiley, 1957).

2. The payoffs I used for the Prisoner's Dilemma were 5 for defecting when the other cooperates, 3 when both cooperate, 1 when both defect, and 0 for cooperating when the other defects. See also xi–xii.

3. Arthur L. Samuel, "Some Studies in Machine Learning Using the Game of Checkers," *IBM Journal of Research and Development* 3, no. 3 (1959): 210–29.

4. Robert Axelrod, "The Evolution of Strategies in the Iterated Prisoner's Dilemma," in *Genetic Algorithms and Simulated Annealing*, ed. Lawrence Davis, 32–41 (London: Pitman, 1987; Los Altos, CA: Morgan Kaufman, 1987.

5. William D. Hamilton, "The Genetical Evolution of Social Behavior, I and II," *Journal of Theoretical Biology* 7, no. 1 (1964): 1–52.

6. Richard Dawkins, *The Selfish Gene*, 4th ed. (Oxford: Oxford University Press, 2016).

7. Adapted from Robert Axelrod, "Agent-Based Modeling as a Bridge between Disciplines," in *Handbook of Computational Economics, vol. 2: Agent-Based Computational Economics*, ed. Leigh Tesfatsion and Kenneth Judd, 1565–84 (Amsterdam: Elsevier, 2006).

8. The quotes from William Hamilton are from his *Narrow Roads of Gene Land, vol. 2*, 118–24 (Oxford: Oxford University Press, 1996).

9. Robert Trivers, *Natural Selection and Social Theory: Selected Papers of Robert Trivers* (New York: Oxford University Press, 2002), 53.

10. Robert Axelrod and William D. Hamilton, "The Evolution of Cooperation," *Science* 211, no. 4489 (1981): 1390–96.

11. Tony Ashworth, *Trench Warfare: 1914–1918: The Live and Let Live System* (New York: Holmes & Meier, 1980).

12. Denise G. Shekerjian, *Uncommon Genius: How Great Ideas Are Born* (New York: Penguin, 1990), xi.

13. Gary King, "Event Count Models for International Relations: Generaliza-

tions and Applications," *International Studies Quarterly* 33 (1989): 123–47; Joshua S. Goldstein and John R. Freeman, *Three-Way Street: Reciprocity in World Politics* (Chicago: University of Chicago Press, 1990); Joshua S. Goldstein, et al., "Reciprocity, Triangularity, and Cooperation in the Middle East, 1979–97," *Journal of Conflict Resolution* 45, no. 5 (October 2001): 594–620.

14. Paul K. Huth, "Extended Deterrence and the Outbreak of War," *American Political Science Review* 82, no. 2 (June 1988): 423–43, quote at 437.

15. Michael P. Lombardo, "Mutual Restraint in Tree Swallows: A Test of the Tit for Tat Model of Reciprocity," *Science* 227, no. 4692 (1985): 1363–65; Federico Sanabria, Howard Rachlin, and Forest Baker, "Learning by Pigeons Playing against Tit-for-Tat in an Operant Prisoner's Dilemma," *Animal Learning & Behavior* 31, no. 4 (2003): 318–31.

16. Lisa K. Denault and Donald A. McFarlane, "Reciprocal Altruism between Male Vampire Bats, Desmodus Rotundus," *Animal Behaviour* 49, no. 3 (1995): 855–56.

17. Marc D. Hauser, "Costs of Deception: Cheaters Are Punished in Rhesus Monkeys (Macaca mulatta)," *Proceedings of the National Academy of Sciences* 89, no. 24 (1992): 12137–39; M. Keith Chen and Marc Hauser, "Modeling Reciprocation and Cooperation in Primates: Evidence for a Punishing Strategy," *Journal of Theoretical Biology* 235, no. 1 (2005): 5–12.

18. Manfred Milinski, "TIT FOR TAT in Sticklebacks and the Evolution of Cooperation," *Nature* 325 (January 19, 1987): 433–35.

19. Adin Ross-Gillespie, et al., "Frequency Dependence and Cooperation: Theory and a Test with Bacteria," *American Naturalist* 170, no. 3 (2007): 331–42.

20. Paul W. Glimcher and Ernst Fehr, eds., *Neuroeconomics: Decision Making and the Brain*, 2nd ed. (London: Elsevier, 2014).

21. Alan G. Sanfey, et al., "The Neural Basis of Economic Decision-Making in the Ultimatum Game," *Science* 300, no. 5626 (2003) : 1755–58.

22. Dominique J. F. De Quervain, et al., "The Neural Basis of Altruistic Punishment," *Science* 305, no. 5688 (2004): 1254.

23. Per Molander, "The Optimal Level of Generosity in a Selfish, Uncertain Environment," *Journal of Conflict Resolution* 29, no. 4 (1985): 611–18.

24. Robert Axelrod, *The Evolution of Cooperation* (New York: Basic Books, 1984), 187.

25. Jianzhong Wu and Robert Axelrod, "How to Cope with Noise in the Iterated Prisoner's Dilemma," *Journal of Conflict Resolution* 39, no. 1 (1995): 183–89. Reprinted in Robert Axelrod, *The Complexity of Cooperation: Agent-Based Models of Competition and Collaboration* (Princeton: Princeton, NJ: Princeton University Press, 1997).

26. Per Molander, "The Optimal Level of Generosity in a Selfish, Uncertain Environment," *Journal of Conflict Resolution* 29, no. 4 (1985): 611–18; Jianzhong Wu and Robert Axelrod, "How to Cope with Noise in the Iterated Prisoner's Dilemma," *Journal of Conflict Resolution* 39, no. 1 (1995): 183–89.

27. Martin Nowak and Karl Sigmund. "A Strategy of Win-Stay, Lose-Shift That Outperforms Tit-for-Tat in the Prisoner's Dilemma Game," *Nature* 364, no. 6432 (1993): 56–58.

28. In their evolutionary simulation, Nowak and Sigmund calculated the success of a strategy based on its long-term average score, which is equivalent to no discounting. The permitted strategies base their choice only on the outcome of the previous move. The strategies are defined in terms of the conditional probabilities to cooperate given the four possible outcomes of the previous move. Most important, perhaps, is the simulation's departure from the evolutionary paradigm in which new strategies are small mutations of current strategies. Instead, the new strategies are drawn from the full range of permissible strategies without regard to the distribution of strategies present in the current population.

29. Anatol Rapoport and Albert M. Chammah, *Prisoner's Dilemma: A Study in Conflict and Cooperation* (Ann Arbor: University of Michigan Press, 1965).

30. Jianzhong Wu and Robert Axelrod, "How to Cope with Noise in the Iterated Prisoner's Dilemma," *Journal of Conflict Resolution* 39, no. 1 (1995): 183–89. We also tried a contrite variant of TIT FOR TAT under the assumption that the noise was due to misimplementation rather than misperception. It also worked well.

31. The second round of the tournament implemented discounting by informing potential entrants that there would be a half-percent chance that each move would be the last.

32. Thomas Hobbes, *Leviathan*, reprinted from the 1651 edition (Oxford: Clarendon Press, 1965), 100.

33. Martin A. Nowak and Karl Sigmund, "Evolution of Indirect Reciprocity by Image Scoring," *Nature* 393, no. 6685 (1998): 573; Manfred Milinski, "Gossip and Reputation in Social Dilemmas," in *The Oxford Handbook of Gossip and Reputation*, ed. Francesca Giardini and Rafael Wittek, 193 (Oxford: Oxford University Press, 2019).

34. D. Hirshleifer and E. Rasmusen, "Cooperation in a Repeated Prisoner's Dilemma with Ostracism," *Journal of Economic Behavior and Organization* 12 (1989): 87–106.

35. Robert D. Putnam, *Bowling Alone: America's Declining Social Capital* (New York: Macmillan, 2000), 223–34.

36. Elinor Ostrom, *Governing the Commons: The Evolution of Institutions for Collective Action* (Cambridge: Cambridge University Press, 1990).

37. Ross A. Hammond and Robert Axelrod, "The Evolution of Ethnocentrism," *Journal of Conflict Resolution* 50, no. 6 (2006): 926–36.

38. Rick I. Riolo, Michael D. Cohen, and Robert Axelrod, "Evolution of Cooperation without Reciprocity," *Nature* 414, no. 6862 (2001): 441.

39. Michael D. Cohen, Rick L. Riolo, and Robert Axelrod, "The Role of Social Structure in the Maintenance of Cooperative Regimes," *Rationality and Society* 13 (2001): 5–32.

NOTES TO PAGES 67–82   151

40. Garrett Hardin, "The Tragedy of the Commons," *Science* 162, no. 3859 (December 13, 1968): 1243–48.

41. Robert Axelrod, "An Evolutionary Approach to Norms," *American Political Science Review* 80, no. 4 (1986): 1095–1111. Reprinted in Robert Axelrod, *The Complexity of Cooperation: Agent-Based Models of Competition and Collaboration* (Princeton: Princeton, NJ: Princeton University Press, 1997).

Part IV

1. Robert M. Axelrod, *Conflict of Interest: A Theory of Divergent Goals with Applications to Politics* (Chicago: Markham Publishing, 1970).

2. The configuration space has sixteen rather than seventeen dimensions to avoid double counting the mirror image of an alignment.

3. Robert Axelrod and D. Scott Bennett, "A Landscape Theory of Aggregation," *British Journal of Political Science* 23, no. 2 (1993): 211–33. Reprinted in Robert Axelrod, *The Complexity of Cooperation: Agent-Based Models of Competition and Collaboration* (Princeton: Princeton, NJ: Princeton University Press, 1997).

4. Robert Axelrod, Will Mitchell, Robert E. Thomas, D. Scott Bennett, and Erhard Bruderer, "Coalition Formation in Standard-Setting Alliances," *Management Science* 41, no. 9 (1995): 1493–1508. Reprinted in Robert Axelrod, *The Complexity of Cooperation: Agent-Based Models of Competition and Collaboration* (Princeton: Princeton, NJ: Princeton University Press, 1997).

5. Robert Axelrod, "The Dissemination of Culture: A Model with Local Convergence and Global Polarization," *Journal of Conflict Resolution* 41 (April 1997): 203–26. Reprinted in Robert Axelrod, *The Complexity of Cooperation: Agent-Based Models of Competition and Collaboration* (Princeton: Princeton, NJ: Princeton University Press, 1997).

6. Ross Hammond and Robert Axelrod, "Evolution of Ethnocentrism," *Journal of Conflict Resolution* 50 (December 2006): 926–36.

7. Robert Axelrod, "The Evolution of Strategies in the Iterated Prisoner's Dilemma," in *Genetic Algorithms and Simulated Annealing*, ed. Lawrence Davis, 32–41 (London: Pitman, 1987; Los Altos, CA: Morgan Kaufman, 1987). Reprinted in Robert Axelrod, *The Complexity of Cooperation: Agent-Based Models of Competition and Collaboration* (Princeton: Princeton, NJ: Princeton University Press, 1997).

8. Benjamin Edwards, Alexander Furnas, Stephanie Forrest, and Robert Axelrod, "Strategic Aspects of Cyber Attack, Attribution and Blame," *Proceedings of the National Academy of Sciences* 114 (March 2017): 2825–30.

9. Robert Axelrod, Joshua Daymude, and Stephanie Forrest, "Preventing Extreme Polarization of Political Attitudes," *Proceedings of the National Academy of Sciences* 118, no. 50 (December 14, 2021).

10. Robert Axelrod, "The Structure of Public Opinion on Policy Issues," *Public Opinion Quarterly* 31 (Spring 1967): 363–71.

11. Robert Axelrod, "Schema Theory: An Information Processing Model of

Perception and Cognition," *American Political Science Review* 67 (December 1973): 1248–66. See also Robert Axelrod, "How a Schema Is Used to Interpret Information," in *Thought and Action in Foreign Policy*, ed. G. Matthew Bonham and Michael J. Shapiro, 226–41 (Basel: Birkhauser Verlag, 1977).

12. Robert Axelrod, ed., *The Structure of Decision* (Princeton, NJ): Princeton University Press, 1976).

13. Robert Axelrod and Larissa Forster, "How Historical Analogies in Newspapers of Five Countries Make Sense of Major Events: 9/11, Mumbai and Tahrir Square," *Research in Economics* 71 (2017): 8–19.

14. Scott Atran, Robert Axelrod, and Richard Davis, "Sacred Barriers to Conflict Resolution," *Science* 317 (August 2007): 1039–40.

15. Scott Atran and Robert Axelrod, "Reframing Sacred Values," *Negotiation Journal* (July 2008): 221–46.

16. John C. Masterman, *The Double-Cross System in the War of 1939 to 1945* (Canberra: Australian National University Press, [1945] 1972)

17. Robert Axelrod, "The Rational Timing of Surprise," *World Politics* 31, no. 2 (1979): 228–46.

18. For details, see Rebecca Grant, "The Bekaa Valley War," *Air Force Magazine* 85 (June 2002): 58–62. See also Benny Morris, *Righteous Victims: A History of the Zionist-Arab Conflict, 1881–1998* (New York: Vintage, 2011), 527–28.

19. Personal communication, December 12, 2021.

20. Robert Axelrod and William Zimmerman, "The Soviet Press on Soviet Foreign Policy: A Usually Reliable Source," *British Journal of Political Science* 11, no. 2 (1981): 183–200. The sources were *Pravda* and *Izvestia*.

21. Robert Axelrod and Rumen Iliev, "Timing of Cyber Conflict," *Proceedings of National Academy of Sciences* 111, no. 4 (January 2014): 1298–1303.

22. John Bohannan, "Cyberwar Surprise Attacks Get a Mathematical Treatment," *Science* (website), January 13, 2014. https://www.science.org/content/article/cyberwar-surprise-attacks-get-mathematical-treatment.

Part V

1. William Hamilton, *Narrow Roads of Gene Land, vol. 2* (Oxford: Oxford University Press, 1996), 560–62 and 601–10.

2. The Red Queen refers to a character in Lewis Carroll's *Through the Looking-Glass* who says you have to run as fast as you can just to stay where you are.

3. William D. Hamilton, Robert Axelrod, and Reiko Tanese, "Sexual Reproduction as an Adaptation to Resist Parasites (a Review)," *Proceedings of the National Academy of Sciences* 87, no. 9 (1990): 3566–73.

4. Robert Axelrod, "Evolving New Strategies," *Genetic Algorithms and Simulated Annealing* 89 (1987): 32–41. Reprinted in Robert Axelrod, *The Complexity of Cooperation* (Princeton, NJ: Princeton University Press, 1997).

5. Adapted from Robert Axelrod, "Political Science and Beyond: Presidential Address to the American Political Science Association," *Perspectives on Politics* 6, no. 1 (March 2008): 3–9.

6. Sabrina L. Spencer, R. A. Gerety, K. J. Pienta, and S. Forrest, "Modeling Somatic Evolution in Tumorigenesis," *PLoS Computational Biology* 2.8 (2006): e108.

7. Douglas Hanahan and Robert A. Weinberg, "The Hallmarks of Cancer," *Cell* 100, no. 1 (2000): 57–70.

8. Robert Axelrod, David E. Axelrod, and Kenneth J. Pienta, "Evolution of Cooperation among Tumor Cells," *Proceedings of the National Academy of Sciences* 103, no. 36 (2006): 13474–79.

9. A. Marusyk, D. P. Tabassum, P. M. Altrock, V. Almendro, F. Michor, and K. Polyak, "Non-Cell-Autonomous Driving of Tumour Growth Supports Sub-clonal Heterogeneity," *Nature* 514 (2014): 54–58; Allison S. Cleary, "Teamwork: The Tumor Cell Edition," *Science* 350, no. 6265 (2015): 1174–75; Allison S. Cleary, et al., "Tumour Cell Heterogeneity Maintained by Cooperating Subclones in Wnt-Driven Mammary Cancers," *Nature* 508, no. 7494 (2014): 113; Francesc Castro-Giner, Peter Ratcliffe, and Ian Tomlinson, "The Mini-Driver Model of Polygenic Cancer Evolution," *Nature Reviews Cancer* 15, no. 11 (2015): 680–85.

10. Personal communication, May 2, 2013.

11. Robert Axelrod and Kenneth J. Pienta, "Cancer as a Social Dysfunction—Why Cancer Research Needs New Thinking," *Molecular Cancer Research* 16, no. 9 (2018): 1346–47.

12. K, J. Pienta, E. U. Hammarlund, J. S. Brown, S. R. Amend, and R. M. Axelrod, "Cancer Recurrence and Lethality Are Enabled by Enhanced Survival and Reversible Cell Cycle Arrest of Polyaneuploid Cells," *Proceedings of the National Academy of Sciences* 118, no. 7 (2021).

13. S. Amend, R. T. Gonzalo, T. K. Lin, L. G. Kostecka1, A. de Marzo, R. H. Austin, K. J. Pienta, "Polyploid Giant Cancer Cells: Unrecognized Actuators of Tumorigenesis, Metastasis, and Resistance," *Prostate* 79, no. 13 (2019): 1489–97.

14. For details, see my website: http://www-personal.umich.edu/~axe/

Part VI

1. Averell Harriman told the Soviet ambassador, Anatoliy F. Dobrynin, "We had the impression that any capital we mentioned would be turned down by Hanoi as a matter of face," *Foreign Relations of the United States, 1964–1968, Volume VI, Vietnam, January–August 1968*, April 24, 1968.

2. Robert Axelrod, "Building a Strong Legislature: The Western Experience" [in Russian], *USA: Economics, Politics, Ideology*, no. 2 (1991): 40–45. Reprinted in English in *PS: Political Sciences and Politics* 24 (1991): 474–78.

3. Matthew Evangelista, *Unarmed Forces: The Transnational Movement to End the Cold War* (Ithaca, NY: Cornell University Press, 2002).

4. Robert Axelrod, "An Evolutionary Approach to Norms," *American Political Science Review* 80, no. 4 (1986): 1095–1111. Reprinted in Robert Axelrod, *The Complexity of Cooperation: Agent-Based Models of Competition and Collaboration* (Princeton: Princeton, NJ: Princeton University Press, 1997).

5 Robert Axelrod and Rumen Iliev, "Timing of Cyber Conflict," *Proceedings of the National Academy of Sciences* 111, no. 4 (2014): 1298–1303.

6. Robert Axelrod, "A Repertory of Cyber Analogies," in *Cyber Analogies*, ed. Emily O. Goldman and John Arquilla (Monterey, CA: Dept. of Defense Information Operations Center for Research, 2014).

7. Thomas C. Reed, *At the Abyss: An Insider's History of the Cold War* (New York: Ballantine Books, 2004).

8. Benjamin Edwards, Alexander Furnas, Stephanie Forrest, and Robert Axelrod, "Strategic Aspects of Cyberattack, Attribution, and Blame," *Proceedings of the National Academy of Sciences* 114 (2017): 2825–30.

9. Robert Axelrod, "How to De-Escalate a Cyber Conflict," in Jai Galliott and Theo Farrell, eds., *Oxford Handbook on Remote War* (Oxford University Press, forthcoming). Available at arXiv:2202.07085.

10. Scott Atran and Robert Axelrod, "Why We Talk to Terrorists," *New York Times*, June 30, 2010, A31.

11. I decided in favor of future audiences and did nothing. The problem reminded me of the time when I decided not to report a lax security officer at the RAND Corporation.

12. M. Mousavi, H. Davulcu, M. Ahmadi, R. Axelrod, R. Davis, and S. Atran, "Effective Messaging on Social Media: What Makes Online Content Go Viral?," *Proceedings of the Web Conference 2022* (WWW'22). Association for Computing Machinery, New York, 2022.

INDEX

Note: Page numbers in italics refer to the illustrations.